I Accuse
the
Council!

I ACCUSE THE COUNCIL!

MARCEL LEFEBVRE

Angelus Press

2915 Forest Avenue | Kansas City, MO 64109

Library of Congress Cataloging-in-Publication Data

Lefebvre, Marcel, 1905-1991
  [J'accuse le Concile. English]
  I accuse the Council / Archbishop Marcel Lefebvre. – 2nd ed.
    p.   cm.
  Originally published: Martigny : Editions Saint-Gabriel, 1976.
  Includes bibliographical references.
  ISBN 0-935952-68-3 (softcover : alk. paper)
  1. Vatican Council (2nd : 1962-1965)   2. Catholic Church – Doctrines
  I. Title
BX830 1962.L4213 1998
262'.52–dc21
                                                          98–35488
                                                          CIP

ANGELUS PRESS

2915 FOREST AVENUE
KANSAS CITY, MISSOURI 64109
PHONE (816) 753-3150
FAX (816) 753-3557
ORDER LINE 1-800-966-7337
www.angeluspress.org

ISBN 978-0-935952-68-1
FIRST ENGLISH EDITION—1982
SECOND ENGLISH EDITION—August 1998
SECOND EDITION, SIXTH PRINTING—April 2018

Printed in the United States of America

CONTENTS

A NOTE TO THE READER

By various means attempts have been made, are being made, and will continue to be made to discredit the value of the stand taken by His Grace Archbishop Marcel Lefebvre. We would be led, above all, to believe that he is a very minor theologian, often passed over and, of course, lacking qualifications. That is why, before becoming acquainted with the pages which follow, it is indispensable to put before the reader the moving testimony of Fr. V. A. Berto, whose eminence as a theologian is well known. Father Berto was the private theologian of Archbishop Lefebvre at the Second Vatican Council and Secretary of the *Coetus Internationalis Patrum* (International Body of Fathers).

In January 1964, the seminary at Ecône, Switzerland, did not yet exist. His spontaneous testimony (extracted from a letter to the superior of a religious institute of women, Jan. 3, 1964), given before all the present controversy had erupted, lends more value to the "interventions" of Archbishop Lefebvre and will make the reader more aware of the theological competence of this courageous archbishop:

> I had the honor, a very great and quite unmerited honor—and I say this before God—to be his theologian. The secrecy to which I am sworn covers the work I did under him, but I am betraying no secret in saying that the Archbishop is far superior as a theologian to me, and would to God that all the Fathers had his knowledge of theology. He had a perfectly reliable and keen theological mind, and his great piety toward the Holy See supplemented his natural ability. This allowed him, even before discursive thought could intervene, to discern intuitively what is and what is not compatible with the sovereign prerogatives of the Rock of the Church.
>
> He in no way resembles the Council Fathers who, as one of them had the effrontery to boast publicly, took from the hands of an "expert" in the very car that was taking them to St. Peter's, the "ready-baked" text of their intervention into the Council hall. Not once have I submitted to him a memorandum, a note, or a draft document, without his having reviewed, revised,

re-thought, and sometimes re-worked it from beginning to end. I have not "collaborated" with him; if such a word existed I would say I have truly "sub-laborated" with him in accordance with my capacity as private theologian and in accordance with his honor and dignity as one of the Fathers of an ecumenical Council, Judge and Doctor of the Faith with the Roman Pontiff.

Finally, all footnotes, except those marked "Translator's note," have been added by a professor at the seminary of Ecône to facilitate the reader's understanding of the text.

PREFACE TO THE FRENCH EDITION

Préface

Rien ne semble plus opportun en ces jours où l'"Affaire d'Écône" pose le grave problème des intentions du Concile Vatican II et de son influence sur l'auto-destruction de l'Église, que de publier des documents rédigés au cours du concile.

Les documents manifesteront avec évidence que des orientations libérales et modernistes se firent jour et eurent une influence prépondérante, grâce au véritable complot des cardinaux des bords du Rhin, malheureusement soutenus par le Pape Paul VI.

Les équivoques et ambiguïtés de ce concile pastoral contenaient le poison qui s'est répandu dans toute l'Église par l'intermédiaire des Réformes et applications conciliaires. De ce Concile est née une nouvelle Église Réformée que S.E. Mgr Benelli appelle lui-même l'Église conciliaire.

Pour bien comprendre et mesurer la nocivité de ce concile il faut l'étudier à la lumière des documents Pontificaux qui mettent les évêques, les clercs et les fidèles en garde contre la conjuration des ennemis de l'Église agissant à travers le libéralisme et le modernisme, et cela depuis bientôt 3 siècles.

Il faut aussi connaître les documents des adversaires de l'Église et spécialement des sociétés secrètes préparant ce concile depuis plus d'un siècle.

Enfin il sera très instructif de suivre les réactions des protestants, des maçons et des catholiques libéraux, pendant et après le concile.

La conclusion s'impose, surtout après l'immense désastre que subit l'Église depuis le Concile; cet événement néfaste pour l'Église catholique et toute la civilisation chrétienne n'a pas été dirigé et conduit par l'Esprit Saint.

Il est rendre à l'Église de Notre Seigneur Jésus Christ + et au salut des âmes un immense service que de dénoncer publiquement les agissements des hommes d'Église qui ont voulu faire de ce Concile la paix de Yalta de l'Église avec ses pires ennemis, soit dans la réalité une nouvelle trahison de Notre Seigneur Jésus Christ et de son Église.

+ Marcel Lefebvre

Écône le 18 Août 1976

Nothing seems more opportune in these days, when the matters at Ecône set forth the grave problem of the intentions of the Second Vatican Council and of its influence on the self-destruction of the Church, than to publish the documents drawn up in the course of the Council itself.

These documents, with supporting evidence, will make it clear that Liberal and Modernist tendencies came to light during the Council and had an overwhelming influence on those present, thanks to the downright plot of the Cardinals from the banks of the Rhine, supported, unfortunately, by Pope Paul VI.

The poison which has spread throughout the whole Church as a result of the reforms of this pastoral Council and of their application is contained in its equivocations and its ambiguities. A new, reformed Church, which His Excellency Cardinal Benelli himself calls the Conciliar Church, has emerged from this Council.

If we are to understand fully and to measure the harm done by Vatican II, we must study this Council in the light of the Pontifical documents which, for nearly two centuries, put bishops, clergy and faithful on their guard against the conspiracy of the enemies of the Church acting through Liberalism and Modernism.

It is also essential to know the documents of the opponents of the Church, and especially of the secret societies which had been preparing for this Council for more than a century.

Finally, it will be very instructive to follow the reactions of Protestants, Masons and Liberal[I] Catholics during and after the Council.

The conclusion is inescapable, especially in the light of the widespread turmoil which the Church has experienced since the Second Vatican Council. This destructive occurrence for the Catholic Church and all Christian civilization has not been directed nor led by the Holy Ghost.

To denounce publicly the machinations of churchmen who sought to make this Council the Church's peace of Yalta with her worst enemies, which is in reality a new betrayal of Our Lord Jesus Christ and His Church, is to render an immense service to Our Lord and to the salvation of souls.

Marcel Lefebvre
Ecône, Switzerland, August 18, 1976

[I] The words "Liberal" and "Liberalism" are used throughout the book in their anti-Catholic context and are not with reference to political parties or to ideologies. (Translator's note.)

Preface to the English Edition

The reader will no doubt find this a difficult book to read. But he will not fail to recognize that the struggle at Vatican II of a small number of conciliar Fathers became, in the long run, the same struggle carried on by the small number of those who resist the world-wide subversion of Socialism and Communism.

The triumph of ecumenical liberalism at the Council was the greatest victory for Communism. Christian civilization forthwith lost its self-confidence and thought it could adopt the principles of its enemies, *viz.* the rights of man, human dignity, and religious liberty. This adoption opened a one-sided dialogue and raised the banner of *détente* and of pacifism. Consequently, Communism has spread over the world without hindrance.

Vatican II, which should have been the anti-Communist Council as the Council of Trent was anti-Protestant, was taken over by the Liberals and became the instrument for the destruction of all the moral and spiritual barriers against Communism. When soldiers have lost the ideal for which they fight their weapons fall from their hands. Since there is no longer a Christian civilization to defend, the field is left open to the Satanic revolution.

In the discussions which appear in these pages, nothing less than the Catholic Faith and the future of so-called Christian nations is at stake. Those who worked to disarm the truth and surrendered it to error bear a heavy responsibility.

May these pages kindle the courage to revive the Catholic Faith for which so many martyrs shed their blood.

May those who contributed so much to this edition be abundantly rewarded. May God recompense them by a wide distribution of this book.

Marcel Lefebvre
Rickenbach, Switzerland
March, 1982

A NOTE ON THE TITLE

Why is this book called *I Accuse the Council?* We have chosen this title because we are justified in asserting—a judgment based on both internal and external criticism—that the spirit which dominated the Council and which inspired so many of its ambiguous, equivocal and even clearly erroneous texts, was not that of the Holy Ghost, but the spirit of the modern world, the spirit of Liberalism, of Teilhard de Chardin, of Modernism, in opposition to the kingdom of Our Lord Jesus Christ.

Submission to the official reforms and orientations coming from Rome is demanded and imposed in the name of that Council. The tendency of all of these, it will be noted, is openly Protestant and Liberal.

It is only since the Council that the Church, or at least churchmen in possession of key posts, has taken a direction definitely opposed to tradition and to the official Magisterium of the Church.

Such men have imagined themselves to be the living Church, and mistress of the truth, with freedom to impose new dogmas advocating progress, evolution, change, and a blind, unconditional obedience on clergy and laity alike. They have turned their backs on the true Church; they have given her new institutions, a new priesthood, a new form of worship, new teachings ever in search of something fresh, and always in the name of the Council.

It is easy to think that whoever opposes the Council and its new Gospel would be considered as excommunicated, as outside communion with the Church. But one may well ask them, communion with what Church? They would answer, no doubt, with the Conciliar Church.

It is imperative, therefore, to shatter the myths which have been built up around Vatican II. This Council had wished to be a pastoral Council because of its instinctive horror for dogma, and to facilitate the official introduction of Liberal ideas into Church texts. By the time it was over, however, they had dogmatized the Council, comparing it with that of Nicaea, and claiming that it was equal, if not superior, to the Councils that had gone before it!

Fortunately, this operation of exploding the erroneous ideas of the Council has already begun, and begun satisfactorily with the work of Professor Salet in the *Courrier de Rome*[2] on the Declaration on Religious Liberty. His conclusion is that this declaration is heretical.

There are a number of points about the Council which should be studied thoroughly and analyzed, for example:

- the questions of the relationship of the bishops and the Pope in the constitutions on the Church, on the Bishops, and on the Missions;
- the priesthood of clergy and laity in the introduction to *Lumen Gentium;*
- the purpose of marriage in *Gaudium et Spes;*
- liberty of worship and conscience and the concept of liberty in *Gaudium et Spes;*
- ecumenism and relations with non-Christian religions and with atheists, *etc.*

A non-Catholic spirit can quickly be discerned in all this. An examination of these points leads us inevitably to look at the reforms which came from Vatican II and suddenly we see the Council in a new and strange light. Then the questions follow: Had those who brought off this astonishing maneuver thought it out in depth before the Council opened? Who are they? Did they get together before the Council?

Gradually one's eyes are opened to behold an astounding conspiracy prepared long beforehand. Such a discovery makes one wonder what part the Pope played in all this work and how responsible he was for what happened. In spite of the desire to find him innocent of this appalling betrayal of the Church, it would seem that his involvement was overwhelming.

Even, however, if we leave it to God and to Peter's true successors to sit in judgment of these things, it is nonetheless certain that the Council was deflected from its purposes by a group of

---

[2]   A bi-weekly publication issued in Paris (14), at 25 rue Jean Dolent. (Translator's note.)

conspirators and that it is impossible for us to take any part in this conspiracy despite the fact that there may be many satisfactory declarations in Vatican II. The good texts have served as cover to get those texts which are snares, equivocal and denuded of meaning, accepted and passed.

We are left with only one solution: to abandon these dangerous examples and cling firmly to tradition, *i.e.*, to the official Magisterium of the Church throughout two thousand years.

We hope that the pages which follow will throw the light of truth on the consciously or unconsciously subversive enterprises of the enemies of the Church.

Let us add that the reactions of Liberal clergy and laity, of Protestants, and of Freemasons to the Council only make our apprehensions stronger. Would not Cardinal Suenens be right in declaring that this Council has been the French Revolution of the Church![3]

Thus our duty is clear: to preach the kingdom of Our Lord Jesus Christ against that of the goddess Reason.

Marcel Lefebvre
Paris, France
August 27, 1976

---

[3] Seventeen eighty-nine was the year of the French Revolution, the year when a statue of the goddess Reason was enthroned on the high altar of Notre Dame Cathedral. (Translator's note.)

Chapter 1

VATICAN II:
THE FIRST SESSION

FIRST INTERVENTION (OCTOBER 20, 1962)

On the Subject of the First Message
Ad Universes Homines

On October 20,[1] at the beginning of the day's session, we were handed a draft message *Ad Universes Homines* [Message to Humanity]—a rather lengthy message which occupied four pages of the Vatican edition of the authentic Acts of the Council.

We were given a quarter of an hour to familiarize ourselves with this. Those of us who wished to introduce any modifications had to inform the Secretariat of the Council by telephone, draft our intervention and present ourselves at the microphone when called by the Secretariat.

It was evident to me that this message was inspired by a concept of religion wholly orientated towards man and, in man, towards temporal advantages in particular, in the search for a theme to unite all men, atheists and religious men—a theme of necessity utopian and Liberal in spirit.

Here are some extracts from this message:

> 1. We as pastors devote all our energies and thoughts to the renewal of ourselves and the flocks committed to us, so that there may radiate before all men the lovable features of Jesus Christ…"that God's splendor may be revealed" (II Cor. 4:6).

---

[1] Pope John XXIII opened the Council on October 11, 1962.

2. The Church too was not born to dominate but to serve.

3. While we hope that the light of faith will shine more vigorously as a result of this Council's efforts, we look forward to a spiritual renewal from which will also flow a happy impulse on behalf of human values such as scientific discoveries, technological advances, and a wider diffusion of knowledge.

4. We carry in our hearts...those who still lack the opportune help to achieve a way of life worthy of human beings.

5. As we undertake our work...we would emphasize whatever concerns the dignity of man, whatever contributes to a genuine community of people.

6. [Two important points: peace and social justice:] This very conciliar congress of ours, so impressive in the diversity of the races, nations and languages it represents, does it not bear witness to a community of brotherly love, and shine as a visible sign of it? We are giving witness that all men are brothers, whatever their race or nation....Hence, we humbly and ardently call for all men to work along with us in building up a more just and brotherly city in this world. We call not only upon our brothers whom we serve as shepherds, but also upon all our brother Christians, and the rest of men of good will....

After this there were only a few rare interventions, one of which, from Bishop Ancel, was accepted; it was a modification of a minor detail.

When I attacked the spirit of this message, I came up against those who had drafted it, and after the session, bitter remarks were addressed to me by His Eminence Cardinal Lefebvre, who had supervised the message, no doubt drawn up by French experts such as Father Congar.

Text of the Intervention (Read publicly)

Venerable Brethren,

In the first place it seems to me that the time allowed for the study and approval of this message was not sufficiently long; in effect it is a message of the greatest importance.

In the second place, and in my humble opinion, it considers primarily human and temporal benefits and does not pay sufficient attention to the spiritual and eternal values; it concentrates on the welfare of the earthly city and takes too little account of the heavenly city towards which we are journeying and for which we are upon this earth. Even though men expect an improvement in their temporal condition through the exercise of our Christian virtues, how much more do they desire, here and now upon this earth, spiritual and supernatural well-being.

Much more could be said about these spiritual values, since they are the true advantages, essential and eternal, which we can and should enjoy even in this earthly life.

In such advantages are peace and blessedness essentially to be found.

SECOND INTERVENTION (NOVEMBER 27, 1962)

On the Purpose of the Council

The ambiguity of this Council was apparent from the very first sessions. What was the purpose of our meeting together? It was true that the discourse of Pope John XXIII had mentioned the way in which he intended to direct the Council, towards a pastoral statement of doctrine (discourse of October 11, 1962). The ambiguity, however, remained, and through the interventions and discussions the difficulty of knowing what the Council was really aiming at could be perceived. This was the reason for my proposal of November 27, which I had already submitted to the pre-conciliar Central Committee[2] and which had collected a large majority of the votes of the 120 members.

We were, however, already far removed from the days of preparation for the Council.

My proposal won over a certain number of votes, among them that of Cardinal Ruffini and of Archbishop (now Cardinal) Roy.

---

[2] The pre-Conciliar Central Committee was created by John XXIII on June 5, 1960, two years prior to the Council, to prepare the draft schemas.

This could have been the opportunity to provide a clearer definition of the pastoral character of the Council. The proposal met, however, with violent opposition: "The Council is not a dogmatic but a pastoral one; we are not seeking to define new dogmas but to put forward the truth in a pastoral way." Liberals and Progressives like to live in a climate of ambiguity. The idea of clarifying the purpose of the Council annoyed them exceedingly. My proposal was thus rejected.

Text of the Intervention (Read publicly)

Venerable Brethren,

Allow me to speak, not only of the schemas but of our method of working.

If we had to leave the Eternal City today to return to our own ministry, would it not be with a certain regret? In fact, even though we may not doubt the existence of a real unanimity among us, such unanimity has so far not been clearly demonstrated.

Does this failure not come chiefly from our method?

Up to now, we have been trying to achieve, in one and the same text, ends which, if not contrary to one another, have been at least very different: notably, to throw light on our doctrine and uproot its errors, to favor ecumenism, to make the truth manifest to all men. We are pastors and, as we are quite well aware, we do not speak the same language to theologians and to the uninitiated; nor do we speak in the same way to priests as to lay people. How then can we define our doctrine in such a way that it will no longer give rise to present-day errors and, in a single text, make this truth intelligible to men not versed in the science of theology? Either our doctrine is not presented to be intelligible to everybody or else it is perfectly well stated, but its formula is no longer intelligible to the uninitiated.

This difficulty has cropped up now in our Council because, with present circumstances and the explicit desire of the Sovereign Pontiff, the necessity of addressing ourselves directly to everybody is more apparent in this than in previous Councils. Perhaps that will be the particular character of Vatican II. Day by day the means of social communication increase our zeal for preaching the truth and our desire for unity.

Moreover, it is clear from the very nature of our subject, as from the words of the Sovereign Pontiff himself, that "it is of the highest importance for an ecumenical Council to conserve and formulate the sacred deposit of Christian doctrine in the most effective manner." And may I be allowed to state, as a Superior General—and I am certain that the other Superiors General are in agreement with me—that ours is a very grave responsibility: that of inculcating in our future priests the love for sound and unerring Christian doctrine. Did not the majority of the pastors here present receive their priestly formation from religious or from members of some clerical institute? For us, then, it is of the highest importance that "the whole of traditional Christian doctrine be received in that exact manner, both in thought and form, which is above all resplendent in the Acts of the Council of Trent and of Vatican I," according to the very words of the Sovereign Pontiff.

So for very important reasons, it is absolutely essential to maintain these two objectives: to express doctrine in a dogmatic and scholastic form for the training of the learned; and to present the truth in a more pastoral way, for the instruction of other men,

How, then, are these two excellent desires to be satisfied? I humbly suggest to you, dear Brethren, the following solution already pointed out by several Fathers.

If I venture to submit this proposal to your judgment, it is for this reason: in the Central Committee we have already experienced the same difficulties, above all in connection with the dogmatic schemas. In order to arrive at a united viewpoint, therefore, I submitted this same proposal to the Fathers of the Central Commission, where it won virtually unanimous approval.

It would seem that this solution, so far proposed only to the Central Commission, should now be extended to all the Commissions. The results would surely be excellent.

The suggestion is this: that each Commission should put forward two documents, one more dogmatic, for the use of theologians; the other more pastoral in tone, for the use of others, whether Catholic, non-Catholic or non-Christian.

Thus many of the present difficulties may find an excellent and really effective solution.

1. There would no longer be any reason to bring forward as objections either doctrinal weakness or pastoral weakness, objections which cause such serious difficulties.

By this means, the dogmatic documents which are thought out and drawn up so carefully and which are so useful for putting the truth before our beloved clergy and for professors and theologians in particular, would still remain as the golden rule of the Faith. There is no doubt that the Fathers of the Council would willingly accept these documents, this holy teaching so expressed.

In the same way the pastoral documents, which lend themselves much more easily to translation into the various national languages, could present the truth in a way that is more intelligible to all men, some of whom may be versed in non-religious branches of learning, but not in theology. With what gratitude would all men receive the light of truth from the Council!

2. The objection to the multiplicity of schemas for the same subject would thus be automatically removed. For instance: the dogmatic schema on the Church's Obligation to Preach the Gospel would be merged with the principles set forth in the schemas on the missions and would become a doctrinal statement for the Commission on the Missions. The schema on the Missions, then, would be a pastoral document, a kind of pastoral guide for all interested in the missions.

The dogmatic schema on the Laity and that entitled *Chastity, Marriage, the Family, and Virginity* would be combined, and two documents would result: the one dogmatic and doctrinal, intended more for pastors and theologians; the other pastoral, for the instruction of the laity.

The procedure would be the same for all the Commissions.

In my humble opinion, if this suggestion were admitted, unanimity would be more easily realized, everyone would receive the best fruits from the Council, and we ourselves could return each to his own ministry, forming but one heart and one soul and with a mind at peace.

I submit this humble suggestion to the wise judgment of the presidency of the Council.

Chapter 2

VATICAN II:
THE SECOND SESSION

THIRD INTERVENTION (OCTOBER 1963)

Intervention Connected with the Notion of "Collegiality" in the Schema on the Church, Chapter 2

This third intervention related to the question of *collegiality*, which some wanted to introduce into the Church's doctrine concerning the relative powers of the Pope and bishops. The term "college" had already been in use in the Church for many centuries, but all those who used it readily admitted that it meant a college of a particular nature.

The attempt to apply the term "collegiality" to the relations which united the Pope and the bishops meant that an abstract and generic notion was being applied to a particular college. The "college" was in danger of no longer being considered as a particular college having an individual at its head, a person with full power vested in himself. Instead the tendency would be to diminish the autonomy of this power and to make it dependent in its exercise on the other members.

It was clear that this was the aim envisaged—to set up a permanent collegiality which would force the Pope to act only when surrounded by a senate sharing in his power in an habitual and permanent way. This was, in fact, to diminish the exercise of the power of the Pope.

The Church's doctrine, on the other hand, states that for the College to be qualified to act as a college with the Pope, it must be invited by the Pope himself to meet and act with him. This has, in fact, only occurred in the Councils, which have been exceptional events.

Hence the emphatic interventions which occurred, in particular that of Bishop Carli.

Text of the Intervention (Read publicly)

Venerable Brethren,

I am speaking on behalf of several Fathers, whose names I am handing to the General Secretariat.

It has seemed to us that if the text of Chapter 2, Nos. 16 and 17, be retained as it is at present, the pastoral intention of the Council may be placed in grave danger.[1]

This text, in fact, claims that the members of the College of Bishops possess a right of government, either with the Sovereign Pontiff over the universal Church or with the other bishops over the various dioceses.

From a practical point of view, collegiality would exist, both through an international Senate residing in Rome and governing the universal Church with the Sovereign Pontiff, and through the national Assemblies of Bishops possessing true rights and duties in all the dioceses of one particular nation.

In this way national or international Colleges would gradually take the place in the Church of the personal government of a single Pastor. Several Fathers have mentioned the danger of a lessening of the power of the Sovereign Pontiff, and we are fully in agreement with them. But we foresee another danger, even more serious, if possible: the threat of the gradual disappearance of the essential character of the bishops, namely that they are "true pastors, each one of whom feeds and governs his own flock, entrusted to him in accordance with a power proper to him alone, directly and fully contained in his Order." The national assemblies with their commissions would soon—and unconsciously—be feeding and governing all the flocks, so that the priests as well as the laity would find themselves placed between these two pastors: the bishop, whose authority would be theoretical, and the assembly with its commissions, which would, in fact, hold the exercise of that authority. We could bring forward many examples of difficul-

---

[1] Cf. the definitive text of the Constitution *Lumen Gentium,* Nos. 22-23.

ties in which priests and people, and even bishops find themselves at variance.

It was certainly Our Lord's will to found particular churches on the person of their pastor, of whom He spoke so eloquently. The universal Tradition of the Church also teaches us this, as is shown by the great beauty of the liturgy of episcopal consecration.

That is why the episcopal assemblies, based upon a moral collegiality, upon brotherly love and mutual aid, can be of great benefit to apostolic work. But if, on the contrary, they gradually take the place of the bishops because they are founded upon a legal collegiality, they can bring the greatest harm to it.

In order then to avoid transmitting to colleges the functions of the Sovereign Pontiff and of the bishops, we suggest another text in the place of Nos. 16 and 17, and we submit it to the Conciliar Commission.

(There follows the names of the eight Fathers of the Council who signed this intervention.)

New Text Suggested in the Place of that in Chapter 2, No. 16, p. 27, of the Schema on the Church

No. 16: The Episcopal College and Its Head

According to the Gospel, St. Peter and the other Apostles founded a College, instituted by Our Lord Himself, insofar as they remained in communion among themselves under the authority of St. Peter. Similarly, the Roman Pontiff, Peter's successor, and the bishops, successors of the Apostles, are united among themselves.

Holy Scripture and the Tradition of the Church teach us that only in extraordinary cases did the Apostles and their successors meet together in councils and act as a collegiate body under the guidance of Peter or of the Roman Pontiffs. The Apostles, in fact, fulfilled their mission personally and transmitted their power to their successors as they themselves had received it from Our Lord.

The Holy Council of Trent, basing itself on these sacred traditions, confirms that the Roman Pontiff alone possesses in his own person a full, ordinary episcopal power over the universal Church. As to the bishops, the successors of the Apostles, as true pastors they feed and govern their own flock entrusted to them, each bishop with a personal power, direct and complete, deriving from his sacred consecration.

Thus at times the bishops also, either some of them or all together, upon a summons from or with the approval of the Roman Pontiff, meet as a true and proper College, acting with a single authority to define and rule the interests of the universal Church or of individual churches.

Such is the constant and unanimous Tradition of the Catholic Church, and no one can call it in question. Such is the ineffable and wonderful Constitution of the Church, which has remained unchangeable up to the present day and is destined to remain so up to the end of time, in accordance with Our Lord's promises.

It is true that present circumstances make it advisable for the bishops to meet more frequently, united in the charity of Christ, in order to share in common their thoughts, desires, decisions, and pastoral cares, keeping always perfect unity, however, without diminishing the power of the Roman Pontiff, or that of each individual bishop.

Commentary on the Session by Archbishop Lefebvre

The result of these interventions was an important modification of the text, but it was not yet, however, completely satisfactory. The Holy Father was therefore respectfully urged to make a clear statement which would avoid any ambiguous interpretation of the text. And it was the insertion of the *nota explicativa* that restored the traditional teaching. This note was very unwillingly accepted in Liberal circles. Henceforth it forms part of the *Acts of the Council* and modifies Chapter 2 of the schema *De Ecclesia*.

FOURTH INTERVENTION (NOVEMBER 6, 1963)

On the Schema for the Decree on the Bishops and Government of the Dioceses

This intervention concerned the schema entitled *De Pastorali Munere Episcoporum in Ecclesia*. This schema returned to the relations of the bishops with the Pope and again tried to introduce new formulae which would limit the freedom of the Pope in the exercise of his functions.

In the schema proposed, it was stated on page 6, no. 3, lines 16-20: "The power of the Roman Pontiff remaining unchanged as regards reserving to himself in all things the causes that he himself shall judge fit to retain, whether they come within his jurisdiction of their very nature, or *to keep the unity of the Church....*"

The second reason mentioned here introduced a new element which changed Canon 220 [of the 1917 Code of Canon Law]. The latter says, in effect: "Those causes are called major which because of their importance revert to the Roman Pontiff alone, whether by their nature or whether *by a positive law.*"

Thus, instead of a positive law which is none other than Canon Law, a criterion was introduced which would allow the powers that the Pope reserves to himself—"the guardianship of the unity of the Church"—to be contested.

Moreover, on page 7 of the schema the question arises of the choice of the bishops who could assist the Roman Congregations by their work. A distinctly democratic climate was introduced here: "Bishops of different nations, each designated by his national episcopal conference, shall be nominated by the Apostolic See in the various Congregations."

Text of the Intervention

Venerable Fathers,

The introduction clearly states: "The Second Vatican Council now begins to deal with subjects which are strictly and truly pastoral." Nevertheless, these subjects cannot be studied thoroughly and honestly unless one bases one's examination on definite theological principles.

Thus two statements must be made, in my opinion, about Chapter 1, which deals with the relations between the bishops and the Sovereign Pontiff.

1. As it has been drawn up, this chapter is clearly based—and that most excellently—on principles of divine Catholic doctrine which are certain and already defined, especially by the First Vatican Council.

Furthermore, this chapter is in very close agreement with the words of the Sovereign Pontiff in his recent addresses. Speaking of the bishops associated with him in the exercise of his functions, the Sovereign Pontiff explicitly used the phrase "in conformity with the reaching of the Church and with Canon Law." The judgment of the Sovereign Pontiff in no way postulates a new principle. Canon 230 had already declared: "The Most Reverend and Most Eminent Cardinals form the Senate of the Roman Pontiff and assist him in the government of the Church as his principal counselors and auxiliaries."

Nevertheless, in order to safeguard in every way what are certain basic principles, two amendments seem to me to be essential:

Page 6, line 16: For the words "or to keep the unity of the Church," let the terms of Canon Law, Canon 220, be substituted, "or by positive law."

Page 7, lines 22-23: Let the words "should be designated by the national episcopal conference" be re-worded in order to safeguard fully the liberty of the Sovereign Pontiff in the exercise of his power.

2. As the relations between the bishops and the Sovereign Pontiff must be based upon principles which are absolutely certain, in no way can mention be made of the principle of juridical collegiality. In fact, as His Eminence Cardinal Brown pointed out, this principle of juridical collegiality cannot be proved.

If, by some miracle, this principle should be discovered in this Council, and solemnly affirmed, it would then be logically necessary to assent, as one of the Fathers has almost declared: "The Roman Church has erred in not knowing the fundamental principle of her divine Constitution, namely, the principle of juridical collegiality. And that over many centuries."

Logically, too, it would have to be stated that the Roman Pontiffs have abused their power up to the present day by denying to the bishops rights which are theirs by divine law. Could we not then say to the Sovereign Pontiff what some have said to him in equivalent terms: "Pay what thou owest"?

Now, this is grotesque and without the slightest foundation.

To conclude: if we are speaking of moral collegiality, who will deny it? Everyone admits it. But such collegiality only produces moral relations. If we are speaking of juridical collegiality, on the other hand, then, as Bishop Carli has said so well: "It can be proved neither by Holy Scripture, nor by theology, nor by history."

It is thus more prudent not to have recourse to this principle, since it is by no means certain.

FIFTH INTERVENTION

On the Schema for the Decree on Ecumenism, and Its Appendix, the Declaration on Religious Liberty

In connection with these schemas on ambiguous and delicate themes which can be made the instruments of Liberal and progressive action, it is vital that the first draft, which clearly shows the authors' intentions, should be translated.

We should be particularly aware of the following points: a deliberate attenuation of the distinctions between "the Christian churches," an exaggeration of the spiritual benefits enjoyed by non-Catholic individuals and communities, and a scandalous declaration of the guilt on both sides at the time of the separation and the schism!

That is why I considered it my duty to intervene. The shortness of the time granted to us (ten minutes) did not allow for lengthy elaborations.

The request of Cardinals Bacci and Ruffini was received and the title modified. The title in question was "Of the Principles of Catholic Ecumenism." This was changed to: "Of the Catholic Principles of Ecumenism."

Text of the Intervention

Chapter on Ecumenism "in General"

(This intervention was not read publicly, but was filed with the Secretariat of the Council.)

Venerable Brethren,

Certain of the Fathers here are in agreement with the intention of the schema and all its declarations relating to the interior dispositions desirable with regard to our separated brethren. On our part may we find it possible to exert every permissible effort to persuade these brethren to return to the unity of the Church.

Nevertheless, for many reasons, this schema does not seem to us to favor true unity. That is why, generally speaking, it does not seem to us satisfactory. I will explain.

1. With regard to its very title, we endorse the remarks of their Eminences Cardinals Ruffini and Bacci.

2. In Chapters 1, 2, and 3, the principles set out seem to us to promote a false irenicism,[2] both by veiling the truth and by attributing excessive spiritual gifts to our separated brethren.

    i. In the first place, this is how truths are watered down. It is truly said on page 17, lines 20-24:

> Nothing is more alien to ecumenism than that false irenicism which tampers with the purity of Catholic teaching or obscures its true and certain meaning.

In actual fact, however, the most fundamental truths in this sphere are watered down. For instance:

Page 7, lines 25ff.:

> The truth essential to encourage unity, namely, that the sole and indispensable source of unity is the Sovereign Pontiff, Successor of Peter and Vicar of Christ, is only put forward indirectly and incompletely. Where the Vicar of Christ is, there is the Church of the Apostles. God is One, Christ is One, the Vicar of Christ is One, the Church is One. Now here upon earth, the Vicar of Christ is none other than the Roman Pontiff.

This truth, in itself, forcefully yet gently, attracts souls towards the Church, Bride of Christ and our Mother.

Page 9, line 2: The Church is called "general help to salvation." Now if we refer to the Letter of the Holy Office,[3] we also find this:

---

[2] IRENICISM: promotion of peace among Christian churches in relation to theological differences (Editor's note).

[3] Letter from the Holy Office to the Archbishop of Boston, dated August 8, 1949 (Denzinger-Schönmetzer, *Enchiridion Symbolorum*, 3867).

> That is why no one will be saved who, knowing that the Church was divinely instituted by Christ, still refuses to submit to her, or else denies the obedience due to the Roman Pontiff, the Vicar of Christ. Our Lord indeed not only commanded all men to enter the Church, He also instituted the Church as a means of salvation, without which no one can enter the kingdom of heavenly glory.

It is obvious from this letter that the Church is not seen merely as "a general help to salvation."

ii. Secondly, what is said about the inspiration of the Holy Ghost and the spiritual benefits that separated brethren enjoy, is not expressed clearly and unambiguously.

Page 8, line 33: It is said: "The Holy Ghost does not refuse to make use of these churches and communities." This statement contains error: a community, insofar as it is a separated community, cannot enjoy the assistance of the Holy Ghost. He can only act directly upon souls or use such means as, of themselves, bear no sign of separation.

Many other examples could be quoted, particularly on the subject of the validity of baptism, of the faith of those of whom the text does not speak as it should...but time is pressing us.

iii. In Chapter 5, on "Religious Liberty," the entire argument is based on a false principle. In it, indeed, the subjective and objective norms of morality are considered as equivalent. In all societies, whether religious, civil, or that of the family, the results of this equivalence are such as to show that the principle is clearly false. It is said in connection with this: "The common good will serve as a norm to the authorities." But then, how is the common good to be defined, for this should be wholly based on an objective norm of morality?

To conclude: The first three chapters on "ecumenism" favor a false irenicism; Chapter 5, based on subjectivism, favors indifferentism. Thus we reject this schema.

Commentary on the Session by Archbishop Lefebvre

Numerous interventions took place along the same lines, and the text was somewhat reworded, especially in relation to the Pope. The graces of the Holy Ghost given to these separated communities were spoken of with more discretion. Yet, the idea still remained in the context as a whole. What a difference between this schema and that proposed to the Preparatory Central Commission by Cardinal Ottaviani in 1962:

> The main obstacle to liturgical communion between Catholics and dissidents is the nature of that communion in sacred things by which the children of the Church are united among themselves. In fact, the communion of the members of the Church among themselves is a gift of Our Lord Jesus Christ Himself—a gift, made to His Church alone, by which union in the Faith, under a single pastor, is effected. This is the sign of unity in truth and charity, unity which is none other than that of the Mystical Body, the Church, and which already here upon earth is the image and beginning of the heavenly unity in Christ.
>
> Thus, then, when liturgical worship is carried out by ministers of Christ in the name and at the orders of the Church, the community of the faithful confesses the Church's faith. Active participation in the liturgical functions must be considered as assent to the faith of the Church. That is why active participation by dissident Christians, either in the Church's worship or in the reception of the sacraments, is in a general way inadmissible. It is in effect intrinsically contrary to the unity of faith and of communion, and it obscures the outward mark of unity of the Body of Christ, thus favoring religious indifferentism, interdenominationalism and scandal.

Here are the principles from which clear conclusions emerge: in the Council's schema there were only vague formulae which would permit all the experiments that are most scandalous to the laity.

SIXTH INTERVENTION (NOVEMBER 26, 1963)

On Religious Liberty

No subject came under such intense discussion as that of "religious liberty," probably because none interested the traditional enemies of the Church so much. It is the major aim of Liberalism. Liberals, Masons and Protestants are fully aware that by this means they can strike at the very heart of the Catholic Church. In making her accept the common law of secular societies, they would thus reduce her to a mere sect like the others and even cause her to disappear, because truth cannot surrender its rights to error without denying itself and thus disappearing.

It should be noted that this theme formed the subject of a dramatic debate at the last session of the Council's preliminary Central Commission. In fact, two schemas on the same theme were drawn up: one by the Secretariat for Unity directed by Cardinal Bea, the other by the Theological Commission presided over by Cardinal Ottaviani. The title of the schemas alone is significant: the first was *De Libertate Religiosa,* which is the expression of the liberal thesis; the second *De Tolerantia Religiosa,* merely echoes the traditional teaching of the Church.

The clash between the two Cardinals was not long in coming, and Cardinal Ruffini demanded an appeal to higher authority, in the event the procedure of consulting the members was adopted. It was already possible at that time to have an idea as to who was on the side of maintaining the doctrine of the faith and who considered that modern evolution demanded new attitudes, even if these were to contradict the doctrine and constant Magisterium of the Church.

Given the rejection of all the schemas at the beginning of the Council, and in view of the composition of the Commissions, it was to be expected that Cardinal Bea's thesis would be that of the new schema. The Bishop of Bruges, Mgr. De Smedt, was to make himself outstanding by his aggressiveness and tenacity, supported by Fathers Murray, Congar, and Leclerc.

They took up again in detail the themes of Liberalism, with "human dignity," "conscience," "non-compulsion," taking good care not to define the terms nor to distinguish between interior and external acts, between private and public ones, and confusing psychological liberty with moral freedom.

All this had been studied by the moral theologians and the Canon lawyers. The Sovereign Pontiffs had taken care to make all the distinctions necessary, in particular Pope Leo XIII in his encyclical *Libertas,* and also Pope St. Pius X. But Liberal Catholics have only one aim: to come to terms with the modern world, to satisfy the aspirations of modern man. They no longer have ears for the truth, for common sense, for revelation, for the Magisterium of the Church.

They end up by expressing doctrines which are outrageous. Thus Father Congar, of the Secretariat of the French episcopate, in the Bulletin *Etudes et Documents* of June 15, 1965, wrote:

> What is new in this teaching in relation to the doctrine of Leo XIII and even of Pius XII, although the movement was already beginning to make itself felt, is the determination of the basis peculiar to this liberty, which is sought not in the objective truth of moral or religious good, but in the ontological quality of the human person.

Thus religious liberty no longer is focused in relation to God but in relation to man! This is indeed the Liberal point of view.

The phrase of the schema quoted in the intervention: "The Catholic Church claims as a right of the human person..." is monstrous, and it is odious to credit the Catholic Church with this claim.

Text of the Intervention

Amendment Concerning Chapter 5 on "Ecumenism"
(Filed with the Secretariat, not read publicly)

Venerable Brethren,

All the arguments of Chapter 5 on the subject of "religious liberty" are based on the assertion of "the dignity of the human person." It is said, in fact, on page 4, para. 3:

Thus the man who sincerely obeys his conscience intends to obey God Himself, even though sometimes in a confused way and without knowing it, and that man must be judged worthy of respect.

My pure and simple reply to accepting such a statement as it stands is no. Considering the matter more closely, a distinction must be made: In view of his intention to obey God, yes; in view of his confusion, no.

In view of this confusion, the man is not, and cannot be, worthy of respect.

From where, in fact, does the person derive his dignity? He draws his dignity from his perfection. Now the perfection of the human person consists in the knowledge of the Truth and the acquisition of Good. This is the beginning of eternal life, and eternal life is "that they may know Thee, the only true God and Jesus Christ whom Thou hast sent" (Jn. 17:3). Consequently, so long as he clings to error, the human person falls short of his dignity.

The dignity of the human person does not consist in liberty set apart from truth. In fact, liberty is good and true to the extent to which it is ruled by truth. "The truth shall set you free," said Our Lord, that is, "the truth shall give you liberty." Error is of itself an objective illusion, if not subjective lie. And through Our Lord we also know him who "when he speaketh a lie, he speaketh from his own" (Jn. 8:44). How then is it possible to say of a human person that he is worthy of respect, when he misuses his intelligence and his liberty, even when there is no blame to be assigned to him?

The dignity of the person also comes from the integrity of his will when it is ordained to the true Good. Now error gives birth to sin. "The serpent deceived me," said Eve, who was the first sinner. No truth can be clearer than this to all mankind. It is sufficient to reflect upon the consequences of this error on the sanctity of marriage, a sanctity of the greatest interest for the human race. This error in religion has gradually led to polygamy, divorce, birth control, that is to say, to the downfall of human dignity, above all in woman.

It is thus certain that there is a cleavage between Catholic doctrine and the statements on page 5:

The Catholic Church claims, as a right of the human person, that no one be prevented from carrying out and proclaiming his public and private duties towards God and man...according to the light of his conscience even if it is in error.

The universal order created by God, whether natural or supernatural, is, in fact, in essential opposition to this statement. God founded the family, civil society, and above all the Church, in order that all men might recognize the truth, be forewarned against error, attain to good, be preserved from scandals and thus reach temporal and eternal happiness.

In truth it is opportune to recall the words of Pius IX in his encyclical *Quanta Cura:*

> Contrary to the teaching of the Holy Scriptures, of the Church, and of the Fathers, they do not hesitate to claim that: "the best condition of society is that in which it is not recognized that authority has the power to repress by legal penalties those who break Catholic law, except as far as public peace demands." (Denzinger, *The Sources of Catholic Dogma,* 1689)

To conclude: the chapter on "religious liberty" should be drawn up anew, in accordance with the principle which conforms to Catholic doctrine: "For the very dignity of the human person, error must be repressed to prevent it from spreading, unless a greater evil can be foreseen from its repression than from its toleration."

Remarks Sent to the Secretariat of the Council on the Schema for the Declaration on Religious Liberty (December 30, 1964) (Emended Text)

Chapter 1: General Conception of Religious Liberty

This conception of religious liberty derives its origin and form from an opinion which is nowadays widespread among the public, an opinion founded on the primacy of conscience and freedom from all restraint. These two elements are the essential constituents of human dignity.

Let it be supposed without any proof that "men of the present day are becoming increasingly conscious of the dignity of the human person." How can the Church, without offering explanation or making distinction, admit such a conception as religious liberty?

Is conscience an absolute reality or merely a relative one?

Is conscience the ultimate basis of religion, both objective and subjective?

How can man in following his conscience find his eternal salvation? Is it not because, in objective truth, he finds God and our Savior?

Conscience cannot be defined without relation to Truth, ordained as it essentially is to that quality.

Similarly, human liberty cannot be defined as a freedom from all constraint—otherwise all authority is destroyed. The constraint can be physical or moral. Moral restraint in the religious sphere is very useful and is found through the Holy Scriptures: "The fear of God is the beginning of wisdom."

The purpose of authority is the accomplishment of good and the avoidance of evil, that is, to help men to use their liberty well. The text on pages 3-6 is made obscure by many an equivocation and ambiguity.

The end of the Declaration on page 6 is indeed surprising:

> This Holy Council declares that the present legal administration is worthy of respect in itself and truly essential to the safeguard of human society, both personal and civil, in present-day society.

If such an assertion were true, then the doctrine taught by the Church up to the present time, and above all by the last few Pontiffs, must be false.

It is one thing to state the present need for authority to allow greater liberty and quite another to state that this condition is in fact more in conformity with human dignity. Such a claim would implicitly allow that scandal was admissible, either through error or through vice. God preserve us from this!

Chapter 2: Doctrine of Religious Liberty According to Reason

Integrity of the person (p. 7): How can this principle be put forward? "The link between interior liberty and its social manifestation is utterly indissoluble." What man of common sense can put forward such an assertion without a qualm? What is left of authority or of truth? Moreover, one is asserting that scandal has its rights!

Search for truth: This paragraph clearly shows the unreality of such a declaration.[4] The search for truth, for men living on this earth, consists above all in obeying, in submitting his intelligence to whatever authority may be concerned: family, religious, and even civil. How many men can reach the truth without the help of authority?

Nature of Religion: An inward religion that is erroneous often leads to superstitious external actions contrary to the dignity of man and above all contrary to the dignity of God. Inevitably an erroneous religion carries with it principles contrary to the natural law, above all in the sphere of marriage, as St. Paul says very clearly in his Epistle to the Romans.[5]

How can one say: "It thus follows that man has the right, in the public exercise of his religion, to be utterly free from all coercion, whether legal or social" (p. 8)?

The human conscience: The human conscience[6] is not a blank slate. It contains moral principles, one of which is that "We must obey God and the authorities set up by Him. By divine right the voice of conscience must be subject to authority." Where is conscience to be found, except among men living in society, thus in submission to authority?

---

[4] According to this paragraph it would be in keeping with religious liberty that man, in his search for truth, should not be fettered in his convictions on religious matters, nor in the statement of them which must be made in any "dialogue."

[5] Rom. 1:21-32.

[6] The human conscience is the means by which we judge *hic et nunc* the conformity of our acts with the rule of morality which is the divine law, whether natural (imprinted in every nature which has remained upright, and which is to a large extent the Decalogue), or supernatural (the Gospel). In order to be saved it is not sufficient to follow sincere conscience (which can be in error), but it is essential to form oneself and follow a *true* conscience. An honest civil legislation—which is the application, at the concrete, temporal and natural level, of the principles of natural and supernatural divine law—far from being a danger for the individual conscience is an effective help, willed by God, to enlighten consciences and direct man to his ultimate supernatural end.

Civil Government: Here the statement[7] explicitly contradicts Catholic doctrines[8] (see *Immortale Dei,* Leo XIII[9]).

Limits of Religious Liberty: Unless the "public good" and consequently "public order" are clearly defined, it becomes impossible in

---

[7] The Council's schema (Chapter 2, No. 4c) said this: "Thus the public authority, which cannot judge of internal religious acts [it is true: 'God alone searches the reins and the hearts' (Ps. 7:10)], equally cannot impose [this is true, but not for the same reason] or *prevent* [this is false] *the public* practice of religion [it is wrong not to distinguish the true religion from the false ones] *unless when public order should demand it.*"

[8] In his encyclical *Quanta Cura,* however, Pius IX condemned this proposition expressed in the same terms: "And against the doctrine of Holy Scripture, the Church and the Fathers state without hesitation that the best condition of society is that in which it is not recognized that Authority *has the duty of repressing by legal penalties the violators of the Catholic religion, unless in the measure in which public peace demands it.*"

Certainly public Authority cannot constrain anyone to embrace the Catholic religion (or *a fortiori* another religion) as is stated in the 1917 Code of Canon Law (Canon 1351). But it can on the other hand prohibit or moderate the public exercise of other religions, as explained by Cardinal Ottaviani in his schema on the relations between Church and State, in the following Catholic doctrine: "Just as civil authority deems that it is right to protect public morality, so, in order to protect the citizens against the seductions of error, in order to keep the city in the unity of the faith, which is the supreme good and the source of many benefits even temporal, the civil authority can, of itself, regulate and moderate the public manifestations of other forms of worship and defend its citizens against the spreading of false doctrines which, in the judgment of the Church, endanger their eternal salvation" (introductory schema, *De Ecelesia,* Part 2, Chapter 9, No. 5).

[9] Leo XIII, in his encyclical *Immortale Dei* of November 1885, on the Christian Constitution of the States, after condemning indifferentism on the part of the state in religious matters, sets out precisely the duties of the civil authority in regard to the true religion: "The Heads of State must thus hold as holy the name of God and put in the number of their chief duties that of favoring religion, of protecting it with their goodwill, of sheltering it under the tutelary authority of the law and of enacting or deciding nothing contrary to its integrity....Then, as civil society has been established for the service of all, it must, by favoring public prosperity, provide for the good of the citizens in such a way as not only to place no obstacle against it, but also to ensure all possible facilities for pursuing and acquiring that supreme and immutable good to which they themselves aspire. The first of all these facilities consists in *making the holy and inviolable observance of religion respected,* the duties of which observance unite man to God."

practice to fix the limits of religious liberty. Public good and public order can only be defined in relation to the truth.[10]

Chapter 3: Practical Consequences

The consequences of principles that are equivocal and false cannot be other than equivocal and false.[11]

Chapter 4: Doctrine of Religious Liberty in the Light of Revelation

This doctrine proves nothing "insofar as conscience grasps doctrine."[12]

Holy Scripture can only prove the obligation of submitting to God, to Christ and to the Church, not only one's conscience but one's whole person. One may be unaware of Revelation. One cannot ignore God and the bounden duty of submitting one's person to Him according to the precepts of one's own conscience— precepts which are true and objective, except in the case of certain consciences which are erroneous without any fault on their part.

---

[10] "The temporal common good, the purpose of civil society, is not purely of the material order, but chiefly a moral good" (Leo XIII, *Rerum Novarum*). Moreover, St. Thomas explains that "if men come together in society, it is in order to lead together a *good life*," and this "good life lived in society" he defines as the "virtuous life." Public good and public order are thus defined by St. Thomas in reference to the objective order of the true and the good. The Angelic Doctor goes further: "As (by the free goodness of God) the present life in which we have to 'live well' has heavenly bliss as its purpose, it pertains to the office of the king (or of the public authority) to obtain the good life for the people in general in *the best way for the acquiring of heavenly bliss;* for instance, to *order* (as far as temporalities are concerned) what leads to this heavenly bliss and to *forbid* as far as possible what would be contrary to it" (St. Thomas, *De Regimine Principum*, 1.14). This doctrine the Church has made her own (see *Immortale Dei*).

[11] The schema enumerates four "practical consequences": 1) the religious liberty of the human person must be guaranteed by the civil law (for all religions indiscriminately, be it understood); 2) the liberty of religious communities in the exercise of their worship; 3) the religious liberty of the family; 4) the liberty of religious association.

[12] To repeat the exact phrase of the schema!

Nowhere and to no one does Holy Scripture make scandal permissible, even in the case of a conscience that is erroneous through no fault of its own. Moreover no one can be saved by error, but only by the will to obey God.

Conclusion

It is thus recognized that men of the present day, whatever may be the fundamental formation they have had, daily wish more and more to be able to profess their religion freely, in private and in public....Greeting with a heart full of joy these favorable signs that the present times offer...[i]t is therefore essential that in all places liberty be protected by an effective juridical guarantee....

What does this amount to? What does this conclusion mean?

That each man should remain undisturbed in his own good faith! That a civil society endowed with Catholic legislation shall no longer exist!

That Catholic citizens shall make no attempt at all to resuscitate a Catholic civil society!

That all the moral laws of the various religious communities shall be placed on an equal footing in the civil code, in particular the laws concerning marriage and the use of marriage.

That Catholic schools shall be open to all religions without distinction!

If we admit this conclusion as a doctrine of the Church, we are also admitting doctrinal relativism, practical indifferentism, and the disappearance in the Church of the missionary spirit for the conversion of souls.

The Church's whole vitality comes to her from the Gospel, from the fact that she has always proclaimed herself the only Church founded by Christ for the spreading of truth throughout the whole world, according to Christ's saying: "For this was I born, and for this came I into the world: that I should give testimony to the truth" (Jn. 18:37).

All who come to the Church come to her because she possesses the truth. They accept many sacrifices to obey the truth, to live in the truth.

What is the purpose of these sacrifices? What is the purpose of clerical celibacy? of the virginity of religious of both sexes? What is the purpose of the blood shed by missionaries unless it is shed for the truth, because Christ is the Truth, because Christ's Church is the Truth!

Truth alone is the foundation of right.

Conscience, liberty, human dignity, only possess rights to the extent to which they are in essential relation with the truth.

Notes on the Remarks

These remarks were sent to the Council's Secretariat on December 30, 1964, after being drawn up at Curepipe on the island of Mauritius.

In the face of the difficulties inherent in the improvement of the schema, the Holy Father thought fit to appoint a special commission for the express purpose of studying the suggestions. Three names were put forward for this commission, of which mine was one. It was then that the Cardinals of the Alliance[13] again went to complain to the Pope, who recoiled before this opposition. Apparently what happened was that the other two, one of whom was Cardinal Browne, were appointed to the existing commission. I was the only one eliminated. My interventions on this subject at the Council and my membership of the *Coetus Internationalis Patrum* frightened them.

Nonetheless, it must be recognized that what is in question is a *new doctrine,* contrary to the Canon Law of the Church based on theological principles of defined faith. The statements of Father Congar and Father Murray, who contributed to the draft, are proof of this. See the statements of Father Murray reported by Father Wiltgen in *The Rhine Flows into the Tiber* (p. 248):

> The supporters of what Father Murray called "the most modern theology of religious liberty" were convinced that this liberty was "required by the dignity of the human person." If they

---

[13] The alliance of the bishops from "the banks of the Rhine" or "European alliance."

were in favor of religious liberty, it was not through opportunism, but because, as they believed, it was a question of sound doctrine.

Chapter 3

VATICAN II:
THE INTERMEDIATE SESSION

In preparation for the Third Session, meetings were held at Solesmes. Around Dom Prou were gathered Bishop Morilleau, Bishop Sigaud, and the well-known theologians Dom Frénaud, Canon Berto, who had kindly accompanied me to Rome in the capacity of *peritus*, and myself.

Several important documents emerged from these meetings:

1. A letter to the Holy Father on the danger of the ambiguous expressions often used in the wording of the Council's schemas. It remained unanswered.

2. An important work on the schemas *De Revelatione* and *De Ecclesia* which should be in the hands of all who study the Conciliar texts.

3. A note addressed to the Sovereign Pontiff concerning the first three chapters of the schema *Constitutionis de Ecclesia*. This very complete note on the Apostolic College and Collegiality was drawn up by Cardinal Larraona and signed by certain Cardinals and superiors of religious congregations. I most willingly added my signature to it. It received a reply in the Pope's own hand, utterly disappointing and disconcerting.

Hence the three documents which follow:

1. Letter on the ambiguities.
2. Cardinal Larraona's note.
3. The Pope's reply.

DOCUMENT NO. 1 (JUNE 1964)

Letter Addressed to the Holy Father, Signed by Five Conciliar Fathers, on the Danger of the Ambiguous Expressions

Most Holy Father,

Humbly prostrate at the feet of Your Holiness, we most respectfully beg You to deign to receive the supplication that we venture to address to you.

On the eve of the Council's third session, we are studying the schemas put forward for discussion by, or for the vote of, the Fathers. In the case of certain of these propositions, we have to avow our grave disquiet and our keen anxiety.

In these statements, we find absolutely nothing of what was laid down by His Holiness John XXIII, namely, "that accuracy of terms and concepts which was the particular glory of the Council of Trent and of the last Vatican Council." The confusion of style and of ideas produces an almost permanent impression of ambiguity.

The outcome of ambiguity is to open the door to the danger of false interpretations and to permit developments that are certainly not in the minds of the Conciliar Fathers. Indeed the "formulations" are new and at times completely unexpected. They are so, it seems to us, to the extent that they do not appear to us to preserve "the same meaning and the same bearing" as those which the Church has employed up to now. For us, who have desired to show ourselves obedient to the encyclical *Humani Generis,* our confusion is considerable.

This danger of ambiguity is not illusory. Already the studies made by some of the Council's "experts," addressed to some of the bishops whose advisers they are, reach conclusions which we were always taught to consider as imprudent and dangerous, if not fundamentally false. Certain schemas, and in particular the Decree on Ecumenism and the Declaration on Religious Liberty, are thus exploited, with satisfaction and contentment, in such terms and in such a sense that if they do not always contradict, they are at least formally opposed as much to the teaching of the ordinary Magisterium as to the pronouncements of the extraordinary Magisterium, made by the Church during the past century and more. We can no longer recognize in them either the Catholic theology or the sound philosophy which should light the way for reason.

What seems to us to make the question even graver is that the lack of precision in the schemas appears to us to open the way to ideas and theories against which the Apostolic See has unceasingly put us on our guard.

Finally, we observe that the commentaries made on the schemas under consideration present the questions put forward as if they were all but resolved already. This cannot fail, as we know from experience, to put pressure on the way the Fathers vote.

It is not our purpose to put others in the wrong, but very sincerely to labor for the salvation of souls, which charity can ensure only in the truth.

We beg to add that a large number of priests and lay people to whom an extremely prolific press offers these dangerous perspectives of *aggiornamento* confess themselves as greatly troubled.

It is our prayer, Most Holy Father, made in the most humble submission, that at the opening of the forthcoming labors of the Council, Your Holiness may deign to give a solemn reminder that the Church's doctrine must be expressed unequivocally, that it is by having regard to this necessity that she will bring the new light needed by our times without sacrificing values which she has already bestowed upon the world and without the risk of allowing herself to become a pretext for a resurgence of errors unceasingly reprobated for more than a century.

Begging of Your Holiness the greatest indulgence for the liberty which we have taken, we implore you graciously to accept the assurance of our most filial respect and of our absolute docility, and to have the goodness to give us Your Holiness's blessing.

DOCUMENT NO. 2 (OCTOBER 18, 1964)

Note Addressed to the Holy Father on the Schema *Constitutionis de Ecclesia*

1. In this note—reserved to the Holy Father alone—mention is made of the first three chapters of the schema *Constitutionis de Ecclesia,* and in particular of Chapter 3, *De Constitutione Hierarchica Ecclesiae et in Specie de Episcopatu.* In regard to the first two chapters, *De Ecclesiae Mysterio* and *De Populo Dei,* apart from a few remarks and reservations, we must express our satisfaction at the high quality of the work and at its success. We thus sincerely congratulate the Theological Commission upon it for, in its first two chapters, the Constitution provides a fine description of the Church and of her true countenance, a countenance profound and mysterious.

2. Speaking in all sincerity and loyalty, the judgment we must in conscience bring to bear on Chapter 3, *De Constitutione Hierarchica Ecclesiae et in Specie de Episcopatu,* is very different. While fully recognizing the good it contains, we cannot refrain from expressing serious reservations on this chapter as a whole. Since we loyally believe what we are going to say, we have the right *in Domino*—and not only the right, which we could sacrifice, but the inalienable duty—to make known our fears and our opinions on the subject in the proper quarter.

3. In fact, after careful study, we think it our duty to say in conscience and before God, that Chapter 3:

    i. *As far as doctrine is concerned* brings us:

        a) doctrines and opinions that are new;

        b) doctrines and opinions which are not only uncertain, but not even probable or solidly based on probability;

        c) doctrines and opinions that are often vague or insufficiently clear in their terms, in their true meaning, or in their aims.

    ii. With regard to the arguments put forward, Chapter 3 is:

a) very weak and full of fallacy as much from the historical as from the doctrinal point of view. The proof of this is that those who drew up the final version merely followed the method of excluding from the Biblical Commission's reply to the questions of Your Holiness the words indicating the lack of incontestable scriptural proof of what is put forward;

b) curiously careless of fundamental principles, even of those emanating from earlier Councils or from solemn definitions;

c) so permeated by these faults that an undoubted and readily proved partiality can clearly be seen, stemming from the influence of certain forceful currents that are not doctrinal in their nature, the aims and methods of which are not above reproach;

d) inaccurate, illogical, incoherent and encouraging—if it were approved—endless discussions and crises, painful aberrations and deplorable attacks on the unity, discipline and the government of the Church.

These fears are not based on *a priori* judgments nor are they exaggerated for, unfortunately, as is universally known—since such ideas have been spread by propaganda—even appealing to "the authority of the Council," the sense of discipline has gravely diminished, particularly as regards the statements and dispositions of the Vicar of Christ.

4. The principal points of the schema with which we find ourselves in disagreement or which fill us with grave reservations, concern:

i. the manner of speaking of the Primacy,[1] of its meaning and of its essential purpose;

ii. the power and personal qualities of the Apostles and how far these are handed down to the bishops;

iii. ecumenical collegiality in the case of the Apostles and in

---

[1] The primacy, or pre-eminence of the Roman Pontiff as Successor of St. Peter, was defined by the First Vatican Council (Denzinger, *The Sources of Catholic Dogma,* 1831).

that of the bishops, and territorial collegiality;

iv. the meaning and consequences of a possible Conciliar
declaration on the sacramental nature of the episcopate,
and membership of the "episcopal college" by virtue of
episcopal consecration;

v. the succession of the episcopal college to the Apostolic
College, in the ministries of evangelization, sanctification
and *even of the government of the Universal Church* and
this of divine right;

vi. the power and hierarchy of order and those of jurisdiction.

In the accompanying documents we shall try to make clear at
least briefly, the matters to which we are drawing attention, and to
put forward the pressing theological reasons involved which, not
without cause, awaken our apprehensions.

5. In this document we do no more than stress that:

i. In our opinion, the doctrine set forth and contained in
the schema—as a whole, and, in particular, in the points
enumerated above—is a new doctrine which, until 1958
or rather 1962, represented only the opinions of a few
theologians. Even these opinions were *less common* and
less probable. It was the contrary doctrine which even
recently was *common and encouraged* by the Church's
Magisterium.

ii. The *common* doctrine, accepted in the Church as sound
and more probable until 1962, was *at the root of consti-
tutional discipline and also concerned the essential validity
of acts,* and this as much in the sphere of the Councils,
whether ecumenical, plenary or provincial, as in that of
government (at all stages: pontifical, regional, provincial,
missionary, *etc.*).

iii. The *new* doctrine has become neither more certain nor
objectively more probable than before as a result of the
disturbing campaign of pressure groups who lobbied the
Council in a deplorable way and threw certain bishop-
rics into confusion. Nor has it become more certain as a
result of the actions of many experts who, unfaithful to
their true ministry, made biased propaganda instead of

objectively enlightening the bishops by acquainting them with the *status quaestionis*. And, finally, it has not become more probable through wide coverage of the press which, with its characteristic methods—methods made use of by the Progressives—has created an atmosphere which makes calm discussion difficult, fettering and hampering true liberty by making those who do not show approval appear ridiculous and unpopular. In such an atmosphere scientific argument can no longer exert its legitimate influence in any practical way and is not even given a hearing.

iv. Thus, *the new doctrine is not ripe—either for a Conciliar discussion* which is truly conscientious and exhaustive, and still less for *Conciliar approval*, which can only be granted when there is absolute certainty, when the Fathers are fully aware of the value of certain doctrines and their implications. (Most of the Fathers did not even have the means of acquainting themselves with the true scope of what was being put forward—this because of their inability in practice to follow technical documents, because of the propaganda already alluded to, because of formularies which are inaccurate and not clear, and more-over, because of the fact that the accounts themselves are not fully objective and enlightening, not to mention that they deliberately conceal certain facts). Thus a period of mature consideration is essential on account of the gravity both of the matter under discussion and of the nature of the ecumenical Council.

6. By stressing this last aspect of the need for a period of mature consideration of the new doctrine contained in the schema before the Council could make decisions in regard to it, we wish to emphasize that it would be *new, unheard of* and *exceedingly strange* that a doctrine which, before the Council, was considered less common, less probable, less weighty and less well founded, should suddenly become—particularly because of publicity and not on account of the gravity of the discussions—more *probable*, even *certain*—or truly mature to the extent of being included in

a dogmatic Constitution. This would be contrary to all standard ecclesiastical practice, as much in the sphere of infallible pontifical definitions (cf. Gasser, *Conc. Vat. I*) as in that of non-infallible Conciliar definitions.

If this eagerness to arrive immediately at declarations on these critical questions is intrinsic in the history of the Second Vatican Council, which right from the beginning declared itself opposed to doctrinal definitions, describing itself merely as a pastoral council, it can easily be understood how the total change of attitude in regard to this point is nothing other than a confirmation of the procedures used, that is, of the pressures exerted by certain groups. The latter, feeling themselves in the minority in 1963, wished to exclude the possibility of condemnation, but having acquired an apparent majority by means of non-theological propaganda, now seek to gain their ends at any price. These are the very groups that allowed themselves to criticize the Councils of Trent and Vatican I, accusing them of undue haste and intransigence (!) when, on the contrary, it is well-known that these Councils—especially thanks to the wise procedure of the Congregations of theologians—refrained from concerning themselves with theological doctrines that were no more than probable.

7. Finally, if we consider the gravity of the questions dealt with and solved in this schema, we must weigh their consequences from the hierarchical point of view. Considered thus it may well be said *that the schema changes the face of the Church:*

> i. From being *monarchical,* the Church becomes episcopa-lian and collegiate, and this by divine right and by virtue of the episcopal consecration.
>
> ii. The Primacy is injured and emptied of its content
>
>> a) because, not being based on a sacrament (as the bishop's power is) people logically tend to consider all bishops as equal, by virtue of a common sacrament, and this leads them to believe and state that the Bishop of Rome is no more than a *primus inter pares,* [first among equals];
>>
>> b) because the Primacy is almost solely considered in its *extrinsic function,* or rather, in an extrinsic way in

virtue of the hierarchy alone, only serving to keep it united and undivided;

c) because in several passages of the schema the Pontiff is not presented as the Rock on which the whole Church of Christ, hierarchy and people, rests; he is not described as the Vicar of Christ, who must strengthen and feed his brethren; he is not presented as he who alone has the power of the keys, but he unfortunately assumes the unattractive face of the policeman who curbs the divine right of the bishops, successors of the Apostles. One can easily imagine that this will be the main theme that will be used to claim new rights for the bishops. Moreover, the comment of many of the bishops (who had been influenced by propaganda) when the Holy Father read the Motu Proprio *Pastorale Munus* is well-known: "The Pope is restoring to us—by a kindly concession—part of what he had robbed us of." (The slight emendations made here and there by the Theological Commission, which felt that it was not obliged to accept what the Sovereign Pontiff himself had suggested, do not change the basic meaning of the schema.)

iii. Discipline, and with it Conciliar and Pontifical doctrine, are injured by the confusion between the power of *Order* and the power of *Jurisdiction*. In short, the schema injures the system of Ecumenical Councils, of the other Councils, of Pontifical as well as provincial and diocesan government, of the administration of the missions. It injures the rules concerning the functioning of the power of Order (always valid even if it is illicit) and of the power of Jurisdiction (which can be invalid, even if one has the Order conferring the essential power concerned). Finally, all of this injury is because the distinction between the powers has not been respected, and because account has not been taken of what flows, surely and objectively, from the power of Jurisdiction.

iv. The hierarchy of Jurisdiction, as distinct from that of

Order—which the text declares again and again to be of divine right—is shaken and destroyed. In fact, if it be admitted that episcopal consecration, being a sacrament of Order, brings with it not only the powers of Order (as the ordination of the priest and deacon bestows them in its own degree), but also expressly and by divine right, all the powers of Jurisdiction, of Magisterium and of Government, not only in the bishop's particular church, but also in the Universal Church, it is clear that the objective distinction between the power of Order and that of Jurisdiction becomes artificial—at the mercy of a whim and terribly insecure. And all this—let it be noted—while the sources, the solemn doctrinal declarations of the Council of Trent or more recent ones, the fundamental discipline—all proclaim that these distinctions are of divine right.

The distinction between power and hierarchy of Order on the one hand and that of Jurisdiction on the other is objectively shaken even if one tries to set up "bulwarks" (really futile, however) to save the appearances of the Primacy (at least of what is called the Primacy, *i.e.*, the conventional Primacy, to which certain adherents of modern doctrine refer when they repeat almost word for word the deplorable texts which have already been categorically condemned). Why do we say "to save the appearances of the Primacy"? Because, even if we accept the sincere good faith and the best intentions of those who proposed or accepted these "bulwarks" or limitations, for many others who give a different meaning to the Primacy, considering it purely as *vinculum exterioris unitatis,*[2] the logical consequence will be: if the divine right of the episcopate, as derived from the sacrament of Holy Orders, confers the actual and formal power of Jurisdiction, the latter of necessity follows the norms of the episcopal Order from which it proceeds and is thus always valid in its exercise. The Primacy, on the other hand, which does not come from a sacrament, will be able at most to make the use of jurisdiction *illicit.*

---

[2] "The bond of outward unity." (Translator's note.)

And this will be neither the only nor the final consequence. We have only to think of the repercussions on the greatly desired union with our separated Eastern brethren. This would be logically thought out in accordance with their ideas and thus without full acceptance of the consequences of the Primacy.

We are sure that many of those who have put forward the new theories do not admit these consequences.

They nonetheless do follow logically and strictly from the premises, that is, from the principles contained in the schema. And once the principles have been laid down—and approved—the practical consequences will certainly be drawn from them, despite all the precautions and limitations that have been set up. But, since today there is still time to prevent consequences so disastrous for the Church, it is necessary to foresee what these could be and, going back to the principles from which they spring, to realize that they clearly contain serious gaps, the same as those to which we have drawn attention in the methodology of those who put forward such opinions.

8. Before suggesting a practical solution, as a result of the preceding considerations, we venture to add an extremely important reflection of a theological and historical nature: if the doctrine proposed in the schema were true, the Church would have been living in direct opposition to divine law for centuries! Hence it would follow that, during those centuries, its supreme "infallible" organs would not have been such, since they would have been teaching and acting in opposition to divine law. The Orthodox and, in part, the Protestants, would thus have been justified in their attacks against the Primacy.

In consequence of these considerations, we think it our duty to ask the Holy Father:

    i. To separate from the schema *De Ecclesia* and other schemas based on this part of the latter, all that touches the points we have just enumerated, deferring indefinitely their final discussion and approval. Thus, just as the eighteen years during which the Council of Trent was prolonged (1545-1563) contributed to its complete success—the very pauses, moreover, contributed to the maturing of ideas—a period of waiting would today profit the necessary maturing of the problems raised by the new doctrines. Such a measure would in no way be a suppression of the liberty of the Council or a stranglehold on its free development, but rather a pause which would enable the Council to find its bearings and recover its psychological liberty, which is today nonexistent. If this wise and prudent course were not followed, we might be carried away towards disastrous and highly dangerous solutions.

ii. That, this being done, a complete and technical revision of these matters be proceeded with, a revision which must be made entirely outside the Theological Commission and its environment. This Commission has already given us its finished work. It is natural that the *majority* should defend it energetically, whilst the *minority*—which despite its repeated efforts is not satisfied with it—is in the position of not being able henceforth to do anything. The text should then be submitted to a Congregation of Theologians which, composed of persons of the highest quality, objective and unrelated to the Theological Commission, would make constructive criticism of it.

iii. That this Congregation of Theologians, chosen and appointed by the Holy Father, by his personal mandate, should reconsider the situation in two particulars:

   a) It should take from the schema all that is mature and certain, all that can now be accepted as a positive result of the discussions that have taken place up to the present, and then re-draft Chapter 3 in such a way that the doctrine put forward is fully and in all points in harmony with that defined in previous Councils and contained in the Magisterium. (Such a Congregation of Theologians would thus have a task identical with that of the celebrated Congregations of minor theologians who so largely contributed to the success of earlier Councils.)

   b) It should judge calmly the matters under discussion in order to point out the doctrines that Catholic scholars could accept and those which should be left to research and subsequent discussion, without trying to impose them for non-doctrinal reasons.

iv. This work could be carried out after the Third Session, without fixing the date for the Fourth Session, so that the Holy Father should be completely free to come to a decision in accordance with the course and result of the labors of this Congregation of Theologians.

v. To avoid any unforeseen circumstance which might make it more difficult for the Holy Father to use his absolute liberty in a decision of this importance, it seems to us opportune and even necessary, that such a decision should be taken authoritatively and directly by the Holy Father himself without asking the opinion of the Council and thus without having recourse to voting. Such an act of authority—desired by many—would not only be a practical reaffirmation of the Primacy, but would at the same time promote a more rapid restoration of the balance necessary for progress, and would help us all to become effectively aware of the complexity and gravity of the problems in question.

vi. To facilitate the Holy Father's announcement of such a decision it might be opportune to have drawn up a clear and documented account of the minority point of view: this would indeed give the Holy Father an excellent opportunity of pointing out clearly that the schema, as far as these parts of it are concerned, is not yet either mature or harmonious.

At the same time, the Holy Father would of course be able to appeal to the fact that many Fathers of the Council from all parts of the world have stated their fears and put forward arguments which demonstrate the imprudence of setting out to unbalance questions which are in dispute.

Most Holy Father, we have put forward sincerely and frankly that which in conscience we have deemed it our duty to bring to your notice and which, in our opinion, is of vital importance to the Church, and we are sure that you will see in this approach a fresh sign of our absolute loyalty to your person as Vicar of Christ and to the Church.

At a moment in history which we believe to be grave we place all our confidence in you who have received from Our Lord the charge to "strengthen thy brethren," a charge which you have generously accepted when you said, "We will defend the Holy Church from errors of doctrine and morals which, within and without her boundaries, threaten her integrity and obscure her beauty."

(Drawn up by Cardinal Larraona and signed by several Cardinals and Superiors General including myself)

DOCUMENT NO. 3

The Holy Father's Reply to His Eminence Cardinal Arcadio Maria Larraona, Prefect of the Sacred Congregation of Rites

The "Personal Note" concerning the Conciliar schema *De Ecclesia* has caused Us, as you may well imagine, surprise and concern, as much by the number and high office of the signatories as by the gravity of the objections raised on the subject of the schema's doctrine and of the fundamentally contradictory statements supported, in Our personal opinion, by arguments which are not beyond dispute. Moreover, the "Note" reached Us the night immediately prior to the Third Session of the Second General Vatican Council, when it was no longer possible to submit the schema to fresh examination by reason of the very grave and harmful repercussions, easy to foresee, on the outcome of the Council and hence upon the whole Church, and particularly upon the Roman Church, that the suggestions of the "Note" itself would have had, had they been put into practice.

We have every reason to believe, from what We have been told, that the sending of this document is chiefly due to Your Eminence's initiative, and that not even all who signed it had complete and carefully weighed knowledge of it. Your letter of September 21, on the same theme and with the same purport, followed by another

typewritten text of similar content, gives proof of this. It is therefore to you that We open Our heart, although We do not wish
to give a complete reply to the observations which have been put
before Us, as the opinions of the Council in regard to the schema
in question have already been clearly expressed, and with such a
method of information and voting as to remove all suspicion of
insufficient caution regarding doctrine and the importance of the
different proposals submitted to the vote of the Conciliar Fathers,
and when the examination of the counsels given by the vote *placet
juxta modum*[3] is still in the course of being actively carried out,
inspired as it is by the desire to welcome any reasonable amendment, to dispel certain just fears as to the accuracy of the doctrines
put forward and to reassure all minds.

It seems to Us for the time being adequate and fitting to
inform you, for your peace of mind and in Our own justification,
that We, on Our part, have neglected nothing of what it seemed
right and expedient to do in order that the preparation of the
schema should be carried out in conformity with sound doctrine
and by means of free, calm and objective discussions. We Ourselves
have sought to take account of the controversy relating to certain
affirmations of the schema and of the cogency of the formulae
adopted, consulting both Italian and non-Italian theologians of
excellent reputation and reserving to Ourselves the right to insert
possible amendments after the final text, where orthodoxy or the
clarity of the statement seemed to demand it. We Ourselves have
directed that the Commission *De Doctrina Fidei et Morum* (*i.e.,*
the Commission on the Doctrine of Faith and Morals) should re-
examine the controversial proposals, arranging that the Pontifical
Biblical Commission should pronounce in regard to the exegesis of
certain passages of Scripture cited in the schema in support of the
theories under discussion, thus obliging the Commission *De Doctrina Fidei et Morum* to meet again to re-examine disputed points.
Moreover, it was reassuring to Us to know that the schema, which
had been carefully screened by the Commission in question, and
by the competent sub-commission, had received the explicit approval of His Eminence Cardinal Ottaviani, Secretary of the Sacred

---

[3] "It pleases up to a point." (Translator's note.)

Congregation of the Holy Office, and the even more explicit support of the Assessor of the Holy Office, Monsignor Parente, also a distinguished theologian, not to mention the favorable and almost unanimous vote of the Commission *De Doctrina Fidei et Morum.*

We can assure Your Eminence that the drawing up of the schema is entirely free from the pressures and manipulations to which your statements referred to above attribute its origin.

Neither does it seem to Us that the presentation of the schema in the Council can be charged with undue innovation, as if it had been introduced without due notice when the matter of which it treats is bound up with those of the First General Council of the Vatican, and when its presentation was preceded by a lengthy debate in the first and second sessions of the Council. The General Congregation of the Council on October 30, 1963, had already authoritatively given directions on the line to be taken in this matter, in such a way as to notify each and every one of the Fathers of the Council of the content and importance of the doctrines in question. If there should remain any doubts in this connection, they should easily be dispelled by recalling that detailed pamphlets—authoritative, though without official authorization—had been sent to the Fathers of the Council in support of propositions contrary to those of the schema and had reached the Fathers a few weeks before the re-opening of the Council. It would therefore be almost an insult to their wisdom to suppose that they had no precise knowledge and that they were unaware of the grave and critical doctrinal aspects of the schema.

It appears to Us equally unjustified to state that the majority of the Fathers were subjected to "all kinds of propaganda methods" and that the doctrines in question were "imposed by certain pressure groups who appealed to certain elements of a psychological rather than a theological nature," nor, in fact, do We believe that the fear that the doctrine of the Primacy of the Apostolic See is under attack has any foundation. We think, rather, that we ought to congratulate ourselves on the explicit and repeated professions of deep gratitude and sincere devotion that were made to that Primacy on this solemn occasion.

We can perceive in these serious appraisals and suggestions a noble concern for the orthodoxy of doctrine and a zealous solicitude for Our personal frailty as regards the duties of Our Apostolic office, and for this We are grateful. We shall always be very moved by the appeal made, at such a special time, to Our supreme responsibility, already made watchful by fervent prayers to Our Lord and by the offering of Our unworthy life, that Our testimony may be faithful to the purity of Christ's teaching and to the true well-being of Holy Church. We beg you to believe that We are striving to follow the drawing-up of the final version of the schema with the object of removing from it everything which would appear not to be in conformity with sound doctrine and of making all legitimate emendations to it. We cannot, however, close Our eyes to the fact that new problems in the Church's life may perhaps arise. That will be the responsibility of him whose duty it is to guide her—to keep watch at the head to take care that such problems find favorable solutions, consistent with the fundamental traditions and highest interests of the Church herself. But We have confidence in God's help and are convinced that these solutions will be all the simpler and more useful from the fact that the Roman Curia, ever conscious of its high functions, will have no difficulty in receiving the conclusions of the Council favorably, with readiness and wisdom.

Allow Us in this connection, to beg Your Eminence, and all who have shared your approach to Us, to aid Us always in Our difficult tasks, and to be so good, as to reflect on what disastrous consequences would result from an attitude (if it were not based on true and tested reasons) so contrary to the majority of the bishops and so prejudicial to the success of the Ecumenical Council as well as to the prestige of the Roman Curia.

We ask Your Eminence and all those associated with you to persevere in prayer that the Holy Spirit may assist the Council's great and extraordinary assembly and may deign to guide with His light and His strength him who is the least of all and who has most need of heavenly help, placed as he is by divine ordinance at the head of the Church of Christ in this solemn hour.

With Our respect and goodwill, We also send you on this occasion too, Our Apostolic Blessing.

Paulus P. P. VI

Chapter 4

VATICAN II:
THE THIRD SESSION

SEVENTH INTERVENTION (OCTOBER 1964)

Concerning the Declaration on Religious Liberty

In the course of the Third Session, I presented three interventions, the first of which again dealt with "religious liberty," for, despite the interventions of a number of Fathers, the false fundamental principles remained unchanged.

Text of the Intervention

Venerable Fathers,

This declaration on religious liberty should be shortened, as several Fathers have already said, in order to avoid the controversial questions and their dangerous consequences.

To avoid these dangers, the following remarks seem to me essential:

1. Liberty in our sinful human condition must be clearly defined. Liberty, in fact, is thought of in different ways:
- among the saints,
- among men living upon the earth,
- among the damned.

Liberty is a relative quality, not an absolute one. It is good or bad according to whether it tends to good or to evil.

2. Among the various acts of conscience, the interior acts of religion must be distinguished from the exterior acts, for the external acts can either edify or cause scandal. And which of us

can forget Our Lord's words in regard to those by whom scandals come (Lk. 17:1)?

3. When liberty of external acts is in question, there is also of necessity a question of authority, the function of which is to help men to accomplish the good and avoid the evil, that is, to use their liberty well, in accordance with St. Paul's advice to the Romans: "Wilt thou, then, not be afraid of the power? Do that which is good" (Rom. 13:3).

The declaration against constraint in No. 28 is ambiguous and, in certain respects, false. How does it stand indeed with the paternal authority of the father of a Christian family over his children? With the authority of masters in Christian schools? With the authority of the Church over apostates, heretics, schismatics? With the authority of Catholic heads of state over false religions which bring with them immorality, rationalism, etc.?

4. Attention must be paid to the very grave consequences of this declaration on the right to follow the voice of one's conscience and to act outwardly according to this voice.

And, in fact, a religious doctrine logically influences the whole of morality. Who can fail to see the innumerable consequences of this order of things? Who will be able to determine the dividing line between good and evil when the criterion of morals in accordance with the Catholic truth revealed by Christ has been set aside?

The liberty of all religious communities in human society, mentioned in No. 29, cannot be laid down without at the same time granting moral liberty to these communities: morals and religion are very closely linked, for instance, polygamy and the religion of Islam.

A further grave consequence would be the dwindling of the leading role of the missions and of zeal in evangelizing pagans and non-Catholics, since the voice of conscience of each of them is considered, according to the writer, as a personal calling on the part of Providence.

Who can fail to see the immense harm done to the apostolate of the Church by this statement?

5. This statement is based on a certain relativism and a certain idealism.

On the one hand it considers individual and changing situations of our own times and seeks new guiding lines for our activity, after the manner of those who consider one particular case alone as, for instance, in the United States. But such circumstances can, and in fact do, change.

On the other hand, as this declaration is not based on the rights of truth, which alone can supply a solution that is true and unshakable in every event, we inevitably find ourselves confronted by the gravest difficulties. Moreover, those who drafted this statement are clearly in error in refusing to allow to the Christian heads of state a sense of the truth. Experience proves the utter falsity of such an opinion. In some way or other everyone perceives the truth, those who contradict and persecute true believers, as well as unbelievers who respect the truth and those who believe in it.

In Summary

Should this statement in its present terms come to be solemnly accepted, the veneration that the Catholic Church has always enjoyed among all men and all nations because of her love of truth, unfailing to the point of martyrdom, will suffer grave harm, and that to the misfortune of a multitude of souls whom Catholic truth will no longer attract.

EIGHTH INTERVENTION (1964)

Observations on the Schema on the Missionary Activity of the Church

(Intervention filed with the Council Secretariat)

The second intervention concerned the schema on the Missionary Activity of the Church. This intervention, accompanied with a proposed index, was sent to the Secretariat of the Council.

Text of the Intervention

Venerable Fathers,

Numerous Fathers have already drawn attention to the defects of this schema. In all humility, indeed, I find myself fully in agreement with them.

In its present form, this schema does not correspond to the importance of its subject, an importance, it seems to me, far greater than that of the question of the Church in the present-day world. Moreover, I venture to say that the fundamental answer to the problems of the Church in the present-day world can be found precisely in the Church's missionary activity.

Every day we have experienced this in mission countries. Where the faith and grace of Christ are found, there is also found peace, prosperity, chastity, joy; indeed, all the fruits of the Holy Ghost. Thus I should like to make two observations:

1. In the preamble to the schema, the historic account given by the most eminent exponent who reported on the missionary life of the Roman Church must be summarized. We cannot, indeed, go forward toward the future if we are not supported by the Church's indisputable and glorious tradition.

We must not forget that only the Roman Pontiffs, Successors of Peter, have been able in fact and thus of right, to send missionaries into the whole world. How many Fathers here in this hall have studied here in Rome, in this very city, and have acquired for the whole of their lives a sense of the true meaning of the Catholic Church, and then been sent by the Sovereign Pontiffs into every part of the world, there to found new local churches?

This is because, in fact, only Peter and his successors have possessed this right and duty as part of their ordinary endowment. The other Apostles possessed them only by personal privilege. Thus the bishops, their successors, did not inherit this privilege.

2. On the subject of the international Council in its relationship to the Sacred Congregation for the Propagation of the Faith, extreme prudence must be exercised. It goes without saying that wisdom and prudence demand that the authorities in charge of this matter form their judgment only after consulting men of age and experience. This authority, however, would become ineffective if,

by some means and in some measure, it found itself limited by an assembly endowed with a share of its own authority.

Up to the present and that by right, authority in the Church has been personal, attached to a physical person; it has been a paternal authority, given and received either by a special grace or by a mandate or mission. Such is the fundamental reason for its effectiveness: paternity exercised with the spirit of faith and the help of grace.

Thus it is with prudence that a decision must be made on the subject of this Council in relation to the Sacred Congregation for the Propagation of the Faith.

In Summary

What are the missionary bishops always asking for and demanding from their Superiors General? What do they expect from the propagation of the Faith and from all the bishops of the dioceses? The answer is surely fellow laborers, whether clerical or lay, then financial help, nothing more.

I should like, then, to propose:

1. *On the subject of the fellow laborers:*

a) As far as possible they should be from the same country as the mission. It is a fact of experience that in mission territories, many fine young men can become excellent fellow workers, but find it difficult to achieve the priesthood. If today they could become acolytes, and then, after a fairly long period of probation, unmarried deacons, they could help priests in the parishes considerably. In a few years, there could be very many of them.

b) The bishops of the older dioceses must in no way be afraid to help missionary vocations generously. It is a fact of experience that in a village where a single young man responds to his vocation, he attracts others. Generosity begets generosity. Perhaps, in order to avoid any rivalry in certain regions where vocations have dropped, it might be possible to gather all the young men together into one small seminary and only in the last year to proceed to selection.

2. On the subject of financial help:

I have always been convinced that this question is not insoluble, at least up to a certain point.

If every year each missionary bishop presented a reasonable, precise, and concrete request to the General Council of the Propagation of the Faith, this Council could, through the intermediary of the national president of the Sacred Congregation for the Propagation of the Faith, ask a bishop to choose a certain town or parish of his diocese, making it responsible for a definite work, for which definite jurisdiction would be given. It would be an honor for a town or parish to establish a church or school, or some other religious building in poor regions.

This would perhaps be an excellent opportunity for the episcopal benefactor and a delegation from his diocese to visit this foundation, perhaps on the occasion of its dedication.

It would seem, however, indispensable for everything to be done through the intermediary of the Sacred Congregation for the Propagation of the Faith in Rome and of the diocesan bishop, in order to avoid abuses, and, especially, in order that missionary bishops should no longer have to roam the world over to collect a few thousand dollars and to lose in traveling expenses almost the whole of the sums collected.

To complement all this the indispensable help of prayer must be added. And in order to obtain these prayers for the missions there is room for an association devoted to the promotion of these prayers and to the renewal of their intentions. There is no one, in fact, who does not know that with Christ all things are possible and without Him, nothing.

SUPPLEMENTARY DOCUMENT (1964)

Remarks on the Subject of the Schema on the Missionary Activity of the Church

(Appendices deposited with the Secretariat of the Council)

1. *Importance of the schema.*
2. *The schema in general* contains a serious omission, namely,

that it makes no reference whatever to the ecclesiastical documents, whether of Holy Scripture or of Tradition, which show how, from the beginning and forever, the Church was and always will be, essentially missionary in scope.

3. *The order of subjects in the schema* does not correspond to the real activity of each participant, in line with his true function and responsibility. The order should be as follows:

    i. The Church's right and duty of preaching the Gospel everywhere, especially in the lands where Christ has not yet been made known.

    ii. Duties and rights of the Roman Church, *i.e.,* of Peter's successors and responsibility of all the bishops.

    iii. Manner of carrying out these duties:
- by the Sacred Congregation for the Propagation of the Faith;
- by vows.

4. *Mode of co-operation between the bishops and those dioceses already Christian:*
- To arouse and support missionary vocations
- Financial help
- Through priestly ministry

5. *Missionary religious congregations:*
- Their relations with the bishops in the missions
- Vocations
- The true missionary spirit
- Zeal

6. *The missionaries:*
- Love of the truth, *i.e.,* love of Christ
- Charity and simplicity
- Preaching of the Gospel in the language of the country
- Knowledge of the traditions and customs of the nations to be evangelized
- Schools and institutes for the development of the country in its social capacity

- Vocations of priests, religious, brothers, sisters, and deacons
- Auxiliaries: catechists, associations, Catholic Action
- Evangelization of all men: either by preaching, direct or indirect, or by works of charity, or again by prayer and sacrifice
- Those who listen to the word of God and those who will not heed it

Commentary on the Schema by Archbishop Lefebvre

Numerous remarks might be made on the schema presented to us on the missions. Many missionary bishops concerned themselves with this, but many defects relating to proselytism and to missionary pastoral methods still remain.

One senses the underlying idea that one religion is as good as another.

NINTH INTERVENTION (1964)

On the Schema on the Church in the Modern World

(Intervention filed with the Council's Secretariat)

The third intervention had for its object the Church in the modern world. This had been deposited with the Secretariat of the Council but it was not read publicly.

Text of the Intervention

Venerable Fathers,

In order to effectively reach the aim of the schema on the Church in the Modern World with doctrinal certitude and in a relatively brief space of time (for instance for the next session), I humbly put before you this proposal: What is taken for granted and the general state of the question of the schema present the gravest difficulties because they are vitiated by a certain idealism.

It is thus essential to go back to reality and, as Pope John XXIII wisely remarked: "Do not let us complicate simple things, and if they are complex let us reduce them to simplicity."

First of all, and briefly, we shall speak of what is already taken for granted and of the present state of the problem.

What is taken for granted would appear false: many questions of the world of today, it is claimed, have not, nor have they ever had, any reply on the part of the Church.

Now the essential questions concerning mankind have always had their solution from the world's beginning and, above all, from the time of Our Lord Jesus Christ.

What question of the present day, then, raised in the schema has not yet received a solution, unless perhaps that of the use of marriage in relation to certain quite recent discoveries?

Those who demand answers to such questions from the Church are, I fear, really seeking replies that the Church has already given but which they refuse to accept; like certain writers, Catholic and non-Catholic, they raise the tone of their voice in speaking. Such famous people are "the modern world!" They find or invent a mass of questions with one end in view—that the Church today may contradict her traditional doctrine.

The vocation of the human person, the family, marriage, the social and economic relations between men, civil societies, peace, militant atheism, *etc.*—are all these new questions in the Church? Who will dare to say so!

The supposition then appears to be nothing but the fruit of imagination.

The state of the question, as many of the Fathers have already said, is full of ambiguities, both in the concept of the Church and in that of the world. I now come to the solution which I propose.

Let us return to the Roman Church, Mother and Mistress of all our Churches. In her we must all be united. She alone among all the Churches is indefectible in the Faith.

Let us again listen to the voice of the Sovereign Pontiffs, especially the voice of Pope Pius XII. He is truly, now and forever, the Doctor of the Church in the modern world.

Is there any question pertinent to the present day which that Sovereign Pontiff has not treated? Are we going to maintain that the teachings of that Sovereign Pontiff are no longer suitable for our times?

The work of the Commission will be greatly facilitated if it returns to the teachings of the Sovereign Pontiffs. Why should we neglect this treasure of such great importance?

Would it not be a scandal indeed for all priests, all believers and nonbelievers, if we were to despise all the teachings of the Sovereign Pontiffs, teachings so full of light, which have been proclaimed during the last century, while we are ourselves discussing the same truths and the same subjects? Such an omission on our part would cause grave harm to the Church's Magisterium.

Let us never forget that the Roman Church is our Mother and our Mistress, in accordance with the adage: Rome has spoken, the matter is settled.

Let us be on our guard lest through our passing over these teachings of the Church in silence, the omission may, in the eyes of the whole world, be seen as a lack of devotion and piety towards our Mother and Mistress, resulting in great harm to the Universal Church. "Honor thy father and thy mother and thou shalt be blessed."

Chapter 5

VATICAN II:
THE FOURTH SESSION

TENTH INTERVENTION (SEPTEMBER 9, 1965)

On the Subject of Schema 13 for the Pastoral Constitution on the Church in the Modern World

At the Fourth Session a deeper study of the schema on the Church in the Modern World led me to the discovery that those who had drawn it up lacked the spirit of the Catholic Faith. At least implicitly all the theories of Liberalism and Modernism are to be found in it.

There had been a good deal of opposition to the original text. Yet the very fact that it was possible, unashamedly, to present such a schema to the Fathers clearly demonstrates the progress made by these false ideas in ecclesiastical circles.

Text of the Intervention

Venerable Fathers,

As several Fathers have already declared, it appears to me that it can be stated in regard to this pastoral constitution: The pastoral doctrine presented therein is not in accord with the doctrine of pastoral theology taught by the Church up to the present.

And this is true: Whether it be on the question of man and his condition or that concerning the world and societies, familial and civil, or again on the subject of the Church herself, the doctrine of this Constitution is a new one in the Church, although it has long been familiar to many non-Catholics or Liberal Catholics.

A new doctrine:

1. In various places certain principles are put forward which flagrantly contradict the traditional doctrine of the Church.
2. In many places ambiguous and highly dangerous propositions are affirmed.
3. On essential points many omissions make the true answers to these questions impossible.

1. *In various places certain affirmations contradict the Church's doctrine.* For instance, the Church has always taught, and continues to teach, the obligation for all men to obey God and the authorities established by God in order that they may return to the fundamental order of their calling and thus recover their lost dignity. The schema, on the contrary, says: "Man's dignity is in his freedom of conscience, in his personal actions guided and moved from within himself, that is, of his own volition and not under the compulsion of some external cause or by constraint" (p. 15, lines 15ff.; p. 22, No. 24).

This false notion of liberty[1] and of man's docility leads to the very worst consequences—in particular it leads to the destruction of authority, especially that of the father of the family. It destroys the value of religious life.

Page 18, No. 19: Communism is discussed merely from the point of view of atheism, without any explicit mention of Communism itself. From this text it can be deduced that Communism is condemned solely on account of its atheism. This is clearly contrary to the doctrine constantly taught by the Church.

---

[1] True liberty, befitting the true dignity of the human person, is the faculty that man possesses, enlightened by grace and encouraged by an upright civil legislation, to cling to truth, to practice good, to choose the true religion revealed by God, and to remain attached to it without succumbing to the obstacle of sin and error. Freedom from all external constraint is good if it serves the good, and bad if it is used in the service of evil. Consequently, the Conciliar schemas, putting freedom from constraint in the foreground, invert the values and pervert the sense of liberty which, if it does not lead to good, is nothing.

It is thus better to have a text, it would seem, which either does not mention Communism at all, even indirectly, or which speaks of it, on the contrary, explicitly, to show its intrinsic evil.

Page 39, lines 19ff.: Here it is said: "By His Incarnation the Word of God the Father took upon himself the whole man, body and soul [this is true, indeed]; thereby *He sanctified* all nature created by God, matter included, in such a way that everything which exists, in its own way, calls for its Redeemer."

This quite clearly contradicts not only the traditional teaching but also the universal practice of the Church. If that were true, in fact, what would be the use of exorcisms, of all those things that Christians have for their use? And if the whole of nature is sanctified, why does this not apply to human nature?

Page 47, lines 16ff.: This chapter on marriage presents conjugal love as the primary element of marriage, from which the second element, procreation, proceeds. Throughout this chapter, conjugal love and marriage are made identical, as on page 49, lines 24 and 25. This also is contrary to the traditional teaching of the Church, and if it were admitted the worst consequences would follow. People could say, in fact, "No conjugal love, so no marriage!" Now, there are very many marriages without conjugal love, yet they are genuine marriages.

2. In many places ambiguous, hence dangerous, propositions are affirmed. Page 5, lines 10ff.: "Today, more than in former times, all the inhabitants of the earth, of every race, color, opinion, social origin or religion, must recognize that all men have a common lot, in prosperity as in adversity; that all must take one and the same road towards a goal which has been, up to now, merely glimpsed through shadows."
What does this mean?

The same proposition is repeated at the end of the schema, page 83, lines 35ff.: "Thus doing, we shall lead the whole human race to a lively hope, the gift of the Holy Ghost, that it will finally be admitted one day, for the glory of the Lord, into a world that does not end, into perfect peace and beatitude."

Such propositions demand—it is the least that can be said— greater clarity, if false interpretations of them are to be avoided.

Man's social character is obviously exaggerated. This leads to many propositions that are erroneous in one way or another.

Page 21, lines 23 and 24: "At his death man leaves behind in the world a change, either for the happiness of his brothers or for their misfortune..."

What about the innumerable children who have died before the age of reason?

Page 28, line 16: "No one is saved alone, or for himself alone." As it stands, this proposition simply cannot be admitted!

Where equality among men is spoken of, *e.g.*, pages 25, 30, and 31, many formulae require an explanation before they can be admitted: "Man needs, not only bread, but also respect for his dignity, of liberty and of love." Is such a formula worthy of a Council? It lends itself to many interpretations.

Page 38, lines 22 and 23: The Church is defined thus: "The Church is, as it were, the sacrament of intimate union with God and of the unity of the whole human race." This conception requires explanation: the unity of the Church is not the unity of the human race.

Innumerable propositions contain ambiguities because in reality the doctrine of those who drafted them is not traditional Catholic doctrine, but a new doctrine, made up of a mixture of Nominalism, Modernism, Liberalism and Teilhardism.

3. *Because of many grave omissions, the schema bears the stamp of unreality.* In the introductory statement, pages 6-10, how can one constantly remain silent about original sin with its consequences, and about personal sin, when no valid explanation can be given of the history of the world in general, or of this present world, without reference to the historical fact of original sin and to the present fact of personal sin?

In the chapter on the vocation of the human person, pages 13ff., how is it possible to conceive of man without the moral law? How can one speak of man's vocation, without speaking of baptism and of justification by supernatural grace?

Such omissions are very grave indeed. The doctrine of the catechism would thus have to be revised from top to bottom.

Page 22, line 30; page 48, lines 12-13; page 44, line 19-20: The Church is in no way represented as a perfect society which men are obliged to enter in order to be saved. She is no longer a "sheepfold," since hirelings no longer exist, any more than do thieves or robbers; she is defined as "the evangelical leaven of the whole mass of humanity."

What can be the form, then, of justification for the whole of mankind?[2] External? Internal? All this has the feel of Protestantism.

About the dignity of marriage, the sacrament of matrimony, from which flow innumerable graces for the married couple and the family, is scarcely mentioned. And again, the allusion to the sacrament is defective: "[T]hus, the Savior of men, the Bridegroom of the Church, comes to the meeting of the Christian couple, through the sacrament of matrimony." What does this mean?

Why treat a reality so sacred, so noble, the source of sanctity for the whole of society, in such a terse manner?

In Summary

This pastoral Constitution is not pastoral, nor does it emanate from the Catholic Church. It does not feed Christian men with the Apostolic truth of the Gospels and, moreover, the Church has never spoken in this manner. We cannot listen to this voice, because it is not the voice of the Bride of Christ. This voice is not that of the Spirit of Christ. The voice of Christ, our Shepherd, we know. This voice we do not know. The clothing is that of the sheep. The voice is not the voice of the shepherd, but perhaps that of the wolf.

Commentary on the Schema by Archbishop Lefebvre

Again, it was necessary to return to Religious Liberty, because of the persistence in false doctrine. This persistence in wanting to

---

[2] Justification is the work of divine grace which makes man pass from the state of sin to the state of justice and sanctity. Catholic doctrine, defined at the Council of Trent, holds that justification of the wicked is *internal*—that it truly renews the heart of man. For Protestants, on the other hand, the justified man is not changed, but God no longer imputes his sin to him by reason of the merits of Christ. It is an *extrinsic* justification.

get the Council to accept the Liberal ideas of liberty of thought, liberty of conscience, and liberty of worship was scandalous, and it presented serious problems as to the real worth of the Council. If these theses condemned by the Magisterium of the Church were admitted, this Council would stand self-condemned and would be unable to demand recognition from the faithful.

That was what the group of conservatives thought. That is why they fought on to the end. In the face of this opposition the Pope caused two statements to be added concerning the truth of the Catholic Church and conformity with traditional doctrine. It was this that decided some among us to accept the declaration. Yet nothing in the declaration was changed by these added statements and a good number of the Fathers still voted against it.

ELEVENTH INTERVENTION (SEPTEMBER 1965)

On the Subject of the Declaration on Religious Liberty
(Intervention read at the Council)

Venerable Fathers,

It seems to me that the principles of the Declaration on Religious Liberty could be briefly expressed as follows:

> Founded on the dignity of the human person, religious liberty demands equal rights in civil society for all forms of worship. Society must then be neutral and guarantee the protection of every religion, within the limits of public order.

Such is the conception of religious liberty proposed to us by those who drafted the Declaration.

Is this conception new or has it already received clear support over many centuries? The writer himself has already answered this question. On page 43, he writes: "A fairly long historical evolution, both moral and positive, has led to this conception—which has been in force only since the eighteenth century."

Such an admission destroys *ipso facto* the whole line of argument of the Declaration.

Where, in point of fact, did this conception come into force? In the tradition of the Church or outside the Church? Clearly it made its appearance among the self-styled philosophers of the eighteenth century: Hobbes, Locke, Rousseau, Voltaire. In the name of the dignity of human reason they tried to destroy the Church by causing the massacre of innumerable bishops, priests, religious and laity.

In the middle of the nineteenth century, with Lammenais, the Liberal Catholics attempted to reconcile this conception with the Church doctrine. They were condemned by Pope Pius IX.

This conception, which in his encyclical *Immortale Dei*, Pope Leo XIII calls "a new law," was solemnly condemned by that Pontiff as contrary to sound philosophy and against Holy Scripture and Tradition.

This same conception, this "new law" so many times condemned by the Church, the Conciliar Commission is now asking us, the Fathers of Vatican II, to subscribe to and countersign. It is in the name of this same conception, in the name of the dignity of the human person, that the Communists wish to force all men down to atheism and to justify their persecution of every religion. In the name of safeguarding public order, a number of countries are nationalizing the Church's schools and institutions in order to create political unity.

Jesus Christ Himself was crucified in the name of public order and in the name of that same order, all the martyrs have suffered their tortures.

This conception of religious liberty is that of the Church's enemies. This very year Yves Marsaudon, the Freemason, has published the book *Ecumenism as Seen by a Traditional Freemason*. In it the author expresses the hope of Freemasons that our Council will solemnly proclaim religious liberty. Similarly the Protestants at their meeting in Switzerland are expecting from us a vote in favor of the declaration, without any toning down of these terms.

What more information do we need? As Pope Leo XIII said, this new law tends "to the annihilation of all religions, notably of the Catholic religion which, being the only true one among all of them, cannot be placed on an equal footing with the others without supreme injustice."

In fact, and to sum up, where does the flaw lie in this whole line of argument, impossible as it is to prove by Tradition or Holy Scripture and based solely on reason?

That is why it cannot establish itself by reason: it fails to define the ideas of liberty, conscience, or the dignity of the human person. In fact, to define these notions is to destroy this whole line of argument.

Now, in sound philosophy these ideas are incapable of definition without reference to divine law. Liberty is given to us for the spontaneous observance of divine law. Conscience is natural divine law inscribed in the heart and, after the grace of baptism, is supernatural divine law. The dignity of the human person is acquired by observing the divine law. He who despises the divine law thereby loses his dignity. Do the damned still preserve their dignity in hell?

It is impossible to speak with veracity of liberty, of conscience, of the dignity of the human person except by reference to divine law. This observance of divine law is the criterion of human dignity. Man, the family, civil society, possess dignity in the measure in which they respect the divine law. Divine law itself indicates to us the rules for the right use of our liberty. Divine law itself marks out the limits of constraint permitted to the authorities established by God. Divine law itself gives the measure of religious liberty.

As the Church of Christ alone possesses the fullness and perfection of divine law, natural and supernatural; as she alone has received the mission to teach this law and the means to observe it, it is in her that Jesus Christ, who is our law, is found in reality and truth. Consequently, she alone possesses a true right to religious liberty, everywhere and always.

Other forms of worship, in proportion to their observance of this law after their own fashion, possess—this we can grant—a more or less well-founded title to public and active existence. Where so great a variety of religions exist, it is a matter of investigating particular cases one by one.

Divine law is the key to this whole question of religious liberty, because it is the fundamental norm of religion itself and the criterion of the goodness and dignity of all human activity. We cannot speak of religion if we exclude mention of the divine law. The same principle establishes both the religion and the obligation. Witness the Old Testament and the chosen people, for whom the divine law, engraved on tables of stone, was venerated in the manner of God Himself.

TWELFTH INTERVENTION (OCTOBER 2, 1965)

On the Schema on the Missionary Activity of the Church

Finally, in the face of the danger threatening the Church's missionary spirit, it seemed to me necessary to intervene yet again on the declaration concerning the missionary activity of the Church. It was possible to foresee what would become of the missionary congregations after such directives on liberty of worship and liberty of conscience had been put into effect.

Text of the Intervention

Venerable Fathers,

The new schema on the Missionary Activity of the Church seems to us very much better than the former one, above all, because its object is better defined: "Missions to nations and human communities who have not yet the faith or among whom the Church has not yet sufficiently taken root." These are the words in which the writer has expressed himself.

The order followed in the schema, too, seems more in conformity with truth and reality. Allow me, however, to call attention once again to some very grave defects on points of the greatest importance.

1. Deficiencies in the exact definition of the function of the Sovereign Pontiff and the bishops.

The following passages contain a serious ambiguity and, in some cases, doctrinal novelties.

Page 7, lines 19, 20 and 21: "This function, according to them, the Order of bishops *inherited* with the Successor of Peter...."

On page 25, No. 36, it is stated: "All the bishops were consecrated not only to rule a particular diocese, but for the salvation of the entire world." This implies that the bishops possess jurisdiction over the whole world, which openly contradicts the universal tradition of the Church.

Only Peter and the successors of Peter possess *the strict right* of feeding the whole flock: consequently, the Roman Pontiffs alone possess the right to send missionaries into the whole world. The whole history of the Roman Church proves this very clearly. It is from the Holy See of Rome, the Eternal City, that bishops, priests, and religious are sent into the whole world. It is there that they receive their mandate and their mission. Our schema, however, makes no mention of the constant labor of the Roman Pontiffs for the salvation of the whole human race.

On the other hand and according to *the law*, bishops belong to their diocese, to their own particular flock; then, out of *charity*, they owe their solicitude to every human soul.

Such is the traditional doctrine of the Church, asserted by all the Pontiffs and by the whole of Tradition; by Pope Pius XII again in his encyclical *Fidei Donum*. In fact, all that is mentioned is the obligation for the bishops of solicitude in accordance with the duty of charity.

In his encyclical *Satis Cognitum*, Pope Leo XIII fully expounded this traditional doctrine, clearly set out also in the Constitution *Lumen Gentium* when understood in the light of its explanatory note.

Page 21, No. 27: Another text mentions the general obligation and does not correspond to the doctrine set out in the Constitution on the function of bishops, especially since the decree of the present Sovereign Pontiff on the subject of the Synod of Bishops.

These texts therefore appear to need amendment if they are to accord with the norm of traditional doctrine, particularly a clear statement of the function and rights to that function of the Sovereign Pontiffs and the bishops. An historical reference should be made then to the work of the Roman Pontiffs in the accomplishment of the mandate received from Our Lord.

2. The statement of the aim of missionary activity is also very incomplete. That, too, is very serious, since it is from this statement that vocations must stem and that all missionary activity will be governed.

The statement of the motives for missionary activity, page 9, No. 7, if true, will lead to the withering of every vocation and of all apostolic zeal rather than providing a new stimulus.

The true and essential reason is the salvation of souls through Jesus Christ our Savior, in whose name alone man can be saved, because all men are sinners and remain in their sins if they are deprived of the blood of Christ, which is found truly and fully in the Catholic Church alone.

Not only do we fail to find here the need for the Church and the need for faith and baptism, the need of preaching to accomplish Christ's mission of salvation, but instead and in its place, mention is made of means which depend on the will of God and are foreign to the economy of salvation by the Church.

Indeed, the theology of this fundamental statement of the schema is not traditional. Justification by Christ through the Church appears to be only something better, but not indispensable, as if human nature was not vitiated by original sin and could attain salvation by itself alone because it had remained good. A doctrine like this amounts to a new theology.

As a result, the practice of the apostolate likewise is not traditional. This can be seen by reading Nos. 11, 12, and 13. This direction of the apostolate is based upon principles that are naturalistic and not supernatural. It was not the way Jesus Christ and the Apostles acted. They preached not only to well-disposed souls, as No. 13 states, but to all men, some of whom accepted the Faith, while others refused the Faith and withdrew.

What is wanted is to prepare and train priests who will actively engage in preaching rather than those merely qualified to preach. But who can know if the hearer is well disposed or not? That is the mystery of Christ's grace.

This description should be more closely related to the Gospels and must inspire confidence in supernatural means.

Why is it said on page 13, line 5: "It is forbidden by the Church that anyone should be compelled to embrace the Faith, or be led or cajoled into it by means that are importunate or crafty." This phrase is insulting to missionaries and very far from the zeal for the salvation of souls that we find in the Gospels and in the Acts of the Apostles.

Would that this schema, so important to the Church, could become a source of renewal of the missionary apostolate, since the apostolate is the life of the Church herself!

I am sending in writing to the Secretariat General other remarks of lesser importance.

Additional Remarks to the Secretariat General

Page 7, No. 5: The description of the Church's mission, lines 23-30, would seem inadequate. After the verb "which she brings about"—"through the observance of the orders received" must be indicated. This formula corresponds better to the words of Christ: "Go, therefore, teach ye all nations, baptizing them...and teaching them to observe all things whatsoever that I have commanded you," as was said, moreover, at the beginning.

Page 7, No. 5: A remark of slight importance. Why not say, in line 37: "The blood of the martyrs is the seed of the Church" so that the quotation is authentic?

Page 9, No. 8, lines 49, 50: "That Christ may be...of a new humanity." What new humanity to which the whole world aspires is referred to here? This new humanity would seem to be of this world. Can it then be said that every man aspires to a new worldly humanity as his last end! The text is ambiguous.

Page 12, No. 13, lines 33-39: Here again we do not find the evangelical spirit of preaching. "It is necessary to announce it... to souls...well disposed." Now who can become the judge of the dispositions of souls? And truly, ought preaching to be limited to those who appear in man's judgment to be well disposed? Such a view is in accord neither with the spirit of the Gospel nor with that of faith. "And now, Lord, behold their threatenings..." (Acts 4:29). Apostolic tradition shows us that after a sermon, some go away unbelieving, others on the other hand are converted.

Page 14, lines 17-25: Let us by all means say a few words exhorting people to charity towards Protestants and the Orthodox. But we must avoid in new Christian communities the scandal of indifferentism and the accommodation of the Church towards heretics or schismatics.

Moreover, it is false simply to say "the separated brethren are disciples of Christ regenerated by baptism," since in the majority of Protestant sects, baptism is invalid by defect of form, or matter, or of intention.

If in territories where Christianity has been long established ecumenism is not a source of scandal, among those newly entering the Church a grave danger certainly exists; and among them, in many cases, cooperation with heretics and schismatics will not be looked upon favorably.

Page 16, No. 18 should replace No. 17: Religious do not rank behind catechists.

Page 21, lines 5-6: The reason given here for the existence of institutions seems inadequate. These reasons—religious life, that is, the imitation of Christ; the life of the community and of the family; and thus the greatest effectiveness in the apostolate— should be expressed differently.

Page 23, line 35: It is necessary to suppress the words "and must" as being too imperative an expression.

Page 27, lines 42-43: "...which affect the fundamental struc- tures of social life." These terms are ambiguous. As shown by plain experience, the Church's social doctrine, in particular on the right to private property, results in the greatest economic progress of families among nations whose economy is weak. Socialism, on the contrary, completely stops economic progress among these same nations by the institution of collectivism. We ought therefore to take care in this matter to make deliberate mention of Catholic social doctrine.

Chapter 6

VATICAN II:
AFTER THE FOURTH SESSION

This last intervention brought to an end my direct action at the Council. However, during the Council itself, by letters or by monthly notices addressed to my confreres of the Congregation of the Holy Ghost, I kept them informed. This information has already been published in *A Bishop Speaks*.[1] In these same collected writings is to be found an article intended for publication written during the course of the Council: "In Order to Remain a Catholic, Is It Necessary to Become a Protestant?"[2] The writings in this collection, added to the present disclosure of the interventions, show clearly how grave were the problems with which we were confronted. One would have to be willfully blind not to fear the worst from the consequences of this Council. They have surpassed all the most pessimistic forecasts.

A year after the Council, the faith of many Catholics was so unsettled that Cardinal Ottaviani asked every bishop in the world and all Superiors General of orders and congregations to reply to an enquiry on the dangers which threatened certain fundamental truths of our Faith.

It seems to me to be opportune to make public for posterity the reply which I made as Superior General of the Congregation of the Holy Ghost and of the Sacred Heart of Mary.[3]

---

[1] The English edition of *A Bishop Speaks* is available from Angelus Press.
[2] The French title is *Pour demeurer Catholique, faudrait-il devenir Protestant?*
[3] Generally known as the Holy Ghost Fathers. (Translator's note.)

REPLY TO CARDINAL OTTAVIANI

Rome, December 20, 1966

Your Eminence,

Your letter of July 24, concerning the questioning of certain truths was communicated through the good offices of our secretariat to all our major superiors.

Few replies have reached us. Those which have come to us from Africa do not deny that there is great confusion of mind at the present time. Even if these truths do not appear to be called in question, we are witnessing in practice a diminution of fervor and of regularity in receiving the sacraments, above all the Sacrament of Penance. A greatly diminished respect for the Holy Eucharist is found, above all on the part of priests, and a scarcity of priestly vocations in French-speaking missions: vocations in the English- and Portuguese-speaking missions are less affected by the new spirit, but already the magazines and newspapers are spreading the most advanced theories.

It would seem that the reason for the small number of replies received is due to the difficulty in grasping these errors which are diffused everywhere. The seat of the evil lies chiefly in a literature which sows confusion in the mind by descriptions which are ambiguous and equivocal, but under the cloak of which one discovers a new religion.

I believe it my duty to put before you fully and clearly what is evident from my conversations with numerous bishops, priests and laymen in Europe and in Africa and which emerges also from what I have read in English and French territories.

I would willingly follow the order of the truths listed in your letter, but I venture to say that the present evil appears to be much more serious than the denial or calling in question of some truth of our faith. In these times it shows itself in an extreme confusion of ideas, in the breaking up of the Church's institutions, religious foundations, seminaries, Catholic schools—in short, of what has been the permanent support of the Church. It is nothing less than the logical continuation of the heresies and errors which have been undermining the Church in recent centuries, especially since the

Liberalism of the last century which has striven at all costs to reconcile the Church with the ideas that led to the French Revolution.

To the measure in which the Church has opposed these ideas, which run counter to sound philosophy and theology, she has made progress. On the other hand, any compromise with these subversive ideas has brought about an alignment of the Church with civil law with the attendant danger of enslaving her to civil society.

Moreover, every time that groups of Catholics have allowed themselves to be attracted by these myths, the Popes have courageously called them to order, enlightening, and if necessary condemning them. Catholic Liberalism was condemned by Pope Pius IX, Modernism by Pope Leo XIII, the Sillon Movement by Pope St. Pius X, Communism by Pope Pius XI and Neo-Modernism by Pope Pius XII.

Thanks to this admirable vigilance, the Church grew firm and spread; conversions of pagans and Protestants were very numerous; heresy was completely routed; states accepted a more Catholic legislation.

Groups of religious imbued with these false ideas, however, succeeded in infiltrating them into Catholic Action and into the seminaries, thanks to a certain indulgence on the part of the bishops and the tolerance of certain Roman authorities. Soon it would be among such priests that the bishops would be chosen.

This was the point at which the Council found itself while preparing, by preliminary commissions, to proclaim the truth in the face of such errors in order to banish them from the midst of the Church for a long time to come. This would have been the end of Protestantism and the beginning of a new and fruitful era for the Church.

Now this preparation was odiously rejected in order to make way for the gravest tragedy the Church has ever suffered. We have lived to see the marriage of the Catholic Church with Liberal ideas. It would be to deny the evidence, to be willfully blind, not to state courageously that the Council has allowed those who profess the errors and tendencies condemned by the Popes named above legitimately to believe that their doctrines were approved and sanctioned.

Whereas the Council was preparing itself to be a shining light in today's world (if those pre-conciliar documents in which we find a solemn profession of safe doctrine with regard to today's problems, had been accepted), we can and we must unfortunately state that:

> In a more or less general way, when the Council has introduced innovations, it has unsettled the certainty of truths taught by the authentic Magisterium of the Church as unquestionably belonging to the treasure of Tradition.

The transmission of the jurisdiction of the bishops, the two sources of Revelation, the inspiration of Scripture, the necessity of grace for justification, the necessity of Catholic baptism, the life of grace among heretics, schismatics and pagans, the ends of marriage, religious liberty, the last ends, *etc.*: On all these fundamental points the traditional doctrine was clear and unanimously taught in Catholic universities. Now, numerous texts of the Council on these truths will henceforward permit doubt to be cast upon them.

The consequences of this have rapidly been drawn and applied in the life of the Church:

- Doubts about the necessity of the Church and the sacraments lead to the disappearance of priestly vocations.
- Doubts on the necessity for and nature of the "conversion" of every soul involve the disappearance of religious vocations, the destruction of traditional spirituality in the novitiates, and the uselessness of the missions.
- Doubts on the lawfulness of authority and the need for obedience, caused by the exaltation of human dignity, the autonomy of conscience and liberty, are unsettling all societies beginning with the Church—religious societies, dioceses, secular society, the family.

Pride has as its normal consequence the concupiscence of the eyes and of the flesh. It is perhaps one of the most appalling signs of our age to see to what moral decadence the majority of Catholic publications have fallen. They speak without any restraint of sexuality, of birth control by every method, of the lawfulness of divorce, of mixed education, of flirtation, of dances as a necessary means of Christian upbringing, of the celibacy of the clergy, *etc.*

Doubts regarding the necessity of grace in order to be saved result in baptism being held in low esteem, so that for the future it is to be put off until later, and occasion the neglect of the sacrament of Penance. This is particularly an attitude of the clergy and not of the faithful. It is the same with regard to the Real Presence: It is the clergy who act as though they no longer believe by hiding away the Blessed Sacrament, by suppressing all marks of respect towards the Sacred Species and all ceremonies in Its honor.

Doubts on the necessity of the Catholic Church as the only true religion, the sole source of salvation, emanating from true declarations on ecumenism and religious liberty, are destroying the authority of the Church's Magisterium. In fact, Rome is no longer the unique and necessary *Magistra Veritatis.*[4]

Thus, driven to this by the facts, we are forced to conclude that the Council has encouraged, in an inconceivable manner, the spreading of Liberal errors. Faith, morals and ecclesiastical discipline are shaken to their foundations, fulfilling the predictions of all the Popes.

The destruction of the Church is advancing at a rapid pace. By giving an exaggerated authority to the episcopal conferences, the Sovereign Pontiff has rendered himself powerless. What painful lessons in one single year! Yet the Successor of Peter and he alone can save the Church.

Let the Holy Father surround himself with strong defenders of the Faith; let him nominate them in the important dioceses. Let him by documents of outstanding importance proclaim the truth, search out error without fear of contradictions, without fear of schisms, without fear of calling in question the pastoral dispositions of the Council.

Let the Holy Father deign to encourage the individual bishops of their respective dioceses to correct faith and morals. It behooves every good pastor to uphold the courageous bishops, to urge them to reform their seminaries and to restore them to the study of St. Thomas; to encourage Superiors General to maintain in novitiates and communities the fundamental principles of all Christian asceticism, and above all, obedience; to encourage the development of

---

[4] Mistress of the Truth. (Translator's note.)

Catholic schools, a press informed by sound doctrine, associations of Christian families; and finally, to rebuke the instigators of errors and reduce them to silence. The Wednesday allocutions of the pope cannot replace encyclicals, decrees and letters to the bishops.

Doubtless I am reckless in expressing myself in this manner! But it is with ardent love that I compose these lines, love of God's glory, love of Jesus, love of Mary, of the Church, of the Successor of Peter, Bishop of Rome, Vicar of Jesus Christ.

May the Holy Ghost, to whom our Congregation is dedicated, deign to come to the assistance of the Pastor of the Universal Church.

May Your Eminence deign to accept the assurance of my most respectful devotion in Our Lord.

Marcel Lefebvre
Titular Archbishop of Synnada in Phrygia
Superior General of the Congregation of the Holy Ghost

CONCLUSION

Can it truthfully be said this reply has lost its relevance? It remains as true today as it was yesterday, and the text emphasized remains—alas!—confirmed by the facts. In the course of these ten years we have not had to change our line of conduct.

The criterion of truth and, moreover, of the infallibility of the Pope and of the Church, is its conformity to Tradition and to the deposit of faith. *Quod ubique, quod semper*—That which is taught everywhere and always, in space and in time.

To separate oneself from Tradition is to separate oneself from the Church. It is because it is in the nature of the Church to be a tradition that she has always instinctively had a horror of novelty, of change, of mutation, under any pretext whatsoever. Pope Gregory XVI, in his encyclical *Mirari Vos,*[5] affirmed this:

> Since, to make use of the words of the Fathers of the Council of Trent, it is certain that the Church was instituted by Jesus Christ and His Apostles, and that the Holy Ghost by His daily

---

[5] Available from Angelus Press.

assistance, will never fail to teach her all Truth, it is the height of absurdity and outrage towards her to claim that restoration and regeneration have become necessary for her to assure her existence and her progress.

Marcel Lefebvre